LAST CHAPTER

Also by Ernie Pyle

HERE IS YOUR WAR
BRAVE MEN

LAST CHAPTER

ERNIE PYLE

Last Chapter was originally published in 1946 by
HENRY HOLT AND COMPANY, INC., New York

Last Chapter is part of the
UNCOMMON VALOR REPRINT SERIES

Printed in the United States of America

UNCOMMON VALOR SERIES EDITION
ISBN-13: 978-1537212142
ISBN-10: 1537212141

Contents

LAST CHAPTER

CHAPTER ONE

To the Pacific War

T HE hour of leaving came at last.

When starting overseas, you don't usually get away on the day the transportation people originally set for you. I remember when I first started going to war, how impatient I was at delay, and how I fretted myself into a frenzy over waiting. But time changes things like that. Now, although there was a delay of a few days, I welcomed every one of them with a big embrace. I felt like saying to it, "Ah, my love, you are the day of my dreams. You are my one more day of security – how I cherish you."

But the final day came – early in February 1945 – and at last the hour. I put on my uniform again and sent my civilian clothes to a friend in Los Angeles to keep for me.

It was night when we left San Francisco. We flew in a huge four-motored land plane operated by the NATS (Naval Air Transport Service). The Army's equivalent is the ATC. I've flown on both of them so much I feel like a stockholder. They fly all over the world on clocklike schedule, over all the oceans and all the continents, carrying wartime mail and cargo and passengers. I've flown the Atlantic four times, but this was my first flight across the Pacific. It's nonstop from California to Hawaii, about the same distance as crossing the continent, yet it was as easy as flying from Albuquerque to Los Angeles.

We left shortly after suppertime, and were over Honolulu a little after daylight next morning. Soon after we took off I got some blankets and lay down on the floor in the rear of the plane. When I woke up it was just getting daylight, and we had only an hour to go. That's the way I like to fly an ocean.

All of us had left California in our winter woolen uniforms. When we stepped out of the plane in Honolulu, those heavy clothes almost made us sick. By the time we got through the landing formalities and left the field, we were all dripping and swabbing ourselves.

In Honolulu I stayed in the home of a naval friend. The first thing I did was take a shower, change to light khaki clothes, and eat a plateful of beautiful yellow papaya. A wonderful feeling of tropical well-being came over me. A naval houseboy named Flores, a native of Guam, took care of us. He washed our clothes and made our beds and fixed us fruit juice and papaya all day long. A squat Hawaiian woman, in blue slacks and with a red bandanna around her head, watered the lawn over and over and over again, very slowly. The sun shone bright and white clouds ran an embroidery over the ridges of the far green hills. Palm trees rustled like rain, and the deep whistles of departing ships came from the harbor below us. This, truly, was the Pacific. The trip over had not exhausted me, but the change of climate did, and for a day I did nothing but loaf, and bask in being warm.

Then I started making the rounds to complete my Navy credentials, and to see friends. Lieutenant Commander Max Miller and I stocked up with cigarettes, against the possibility of shortages farther west. Actually we could have bought cigarettes (our favorite brand, too) right downtown in Honolulu. There was no rationing of anything in Honolulu, and no longer any blackout either. Rationing didn't exist because practically everything there was considered military, and also because shipping space from the mainland was an automatic rationer.

The great number of uniforms on the streets and the ten-o'clock curfew were the ever-present reminders of the war; those and the vast growth of construction that had occurred since Pearl Harbor. Otherwise war seemed far away. The grimness of Pearl Harbor

Honolulu was gone. In many respects a newcomer, beguiled by the soft climate and the loveliness of everything, felt more remote from the war than he did back home.

And so I treated my little Honolulu interlude as another reprieve. I sat with old friends; I made a sentimental visit to the small tropical apartment on Waikiki where "That Girl" and I lived for a winter seven years ago; I went to parties and listened almost tearfully to the sweet singing of Hawaiians. I relished the short time there in complacency, and didn't even pretend that I was starting out to report the Pacific war. All that would come soon enough.

Covering this Pacific war was, for me, like learning to live in a new city. The methods of war, the attitude toward it, the homesickness, the distances, the climate – everything was different from what we had known in the European war. At first, I couldn't seem to get my mind around it, or my fingers on it. I suspected it would take months to get adjusted.

Distance is the main thing. I don't mean distance from America so much, for our war in Europe was a long way from home too. I mean distances after you get right on the battlefield. The whole Western Pacific is our battlefield, and whereas distances in Europe are at most hundreds of miles, out here they are thousands. And there's nothing in between but water. A man can be on an island battlefield, and the next thing behind him is a thousand miles away. One soldier told me that the worst sinking feeling he ever had was when, after landing on an island and fighting for three days, he looked out to sea next morning and found it completely empty. The entire convoy had unloaded and left for more and, boy, did it leave him with a lonesome and deserted feeling!

One admiral said that directing this Pacific war was like watching a slow-motion picture. You planned something for months, then finally the great day came when you launched your plans, and then it was days or weeks before the attack happened – because it took that long to get there.

As an example of how they felt, the Navy issued a slick sheet of paper entitled "Airline Distances in the Pacific." And at the bottom of it was printed "Our Enemy, Geography." Logistics out here is more than a word; it's a nightmare. For example, at Anzio in Italy back in February of 1914, the Third Division set up a rest camp for its exhausted infantrymen; it was less than five miles from the front line, within constant enemy artillery range. But in the Pacific, they bring men clear back from the western islands to Pearl Harbor to rest camps – the equivalent of sending an Anzio beachhead fighter all the way back to Kansas City for his two weeks. It's 3,500 miles from Pearl Harbor to the Marianas, all over water, yet hundreds of people travel it daily by air as casually as you'd go to work every morning.

And another enemy out here is one we never knew so well in Europe – monotony. Oh, sure, war everywhere is monotonous in its dreadfulness. But in the Pacific even the niceness of life gets monotonous. The days are warm and on our established island bases the food is good, the mail service is fast, there's little danger from the enemy, and the days go by in their endless sameness and they drive men nuts. It's sometimes called going "pineapple crazy." Our high rate of returning mental cases has been discussed frankly in the island and service newspapers. A man doesn't have to be under fire in the front lines to have finally more than he can take without breaking. He can, when isolated and homesick, have more than he can take of warmth and sunshine and good food and safety – when there's nothing else to go with it, and no prospect of anything else.

Another adjustment I had to make was in the different attitude toward the enemy. In Europe we felt that our enemies, horrible and deadly as they were, were still people. But out here I soon gathered that the Japanese were looked upon as something subhuman and repulsive; the way some people feel about cockroaches or mice. Shortly after I arrived I saw a group of Japanese prisoners in a wire-fenced courtyard, and they were wrestling and laughing and talking just like normal human beings. And yet they gave me the creeps, and I wanted a mental bath after looking at them.

In Honolulu we were far, far away from everything that was home or seemed like home. Five thousand miles from America, and 12,000 miles from my friends fighting on the German border. Twelve thousand miles from Sidi-bou-Zid and Venafro and Troina and Ste.-Mère-Eglise – names as unheard of on the Pacific side of the world as are Kwajalein and Chichi Jima and Ulithi on the other side. The Pacific names were all new to me too, all except the outstanding ones. Those fighting one war do not pay much attention to the other war; each one thinks his war is the worst and the most important war. And unquestionably it is.

We went to the Marianas by airplane from Honolulu. The weather was perfect, and yet so long and grinding was the journey that time eventually became a blur, and at the end I could not even remember what day we had left Honolulu. Actually it was only the day before. We flew in the same kind of plane that brought us from California – a huge, four-motored Douglas transport. As soon as we were in the air Lieutenant Commander Max Miller and I took off our neckties and put on our house slippers. West of Pearl Harbor, military formality immediately dropped away. In Honolulu all naval officers must wear neckties, but the moment they leave Pearl Harbor off they come.

Max and I read awhile in the two books we had brought with us – Thurber's *My World and Welcome to It*, and Joseph Mitchell's *McSorley's Wonderful Saloon*. But good as they both are, we couldn't seem to keep our minds on them, and pretty soon we were more willingly absorbed in a wonderfully informative book the Navy issued to westbound friends, called *Guide to the Western Pacific*.

We made but two stops in the 3,500-mile journey to the Marianas, and how we ever found those two tiny islands is beyond me, for they are the merest dots in the wide ocean. But they find them all the time, so who was I to worry? Our first stop was at Johnston Island, four hours out from Honolulu. As it came into view I was shocked at how small it is – hardly bigger than a few airplane carriers lashed together – and it hasn't a tree on it. Yet it has been developed into an airfield that takes the biggest planes, and several hundred Americans lived and worked there. The climate is magnificent; most of the soldiers and sailors wore only shorts and were deeply tanned. The way I felt, a life of quiet escape there for a while seemed wonderful to me, but the boys were tired of escape, and the monotony of the place got on their nerves. We stopped at Johnston for an hour in late afternoon, then took off and headed west. It was soon dark. One by one the passengers went to sleep in their seats. There was nothing to see out the windows but blackness, and a long night over the Pacific lay ahead of us. The night was extra long, for we were chasing the darkness. The flight orderly brought blankets for everyone, and the passengers wrapped up. But soon most of us unwrapped, for the cabin was heated, and even at high altitude it became almost too hot.

It was after midnight when we could sense by the motors' tone and the pressure in our ears that we were coming down. We couldn't feel the plane turning but it was, for now the moon would be high on one side of u$ and a few moments later it would be low on the other side. Suddenly there were lights smack underneath us, lights of what seemed a good-sized town, and then at last we were on the ground in an unbelievably bustling airport, teeming with men and lights and planes. The place was Kwajalein. (That's not hard to pronounce if you don't try too hard. Just say "Kwa-juh-leen.") It's in the Marshall Islands. There, in March and April of 1944, American soldiers and marines killed 10,000 Japanese, and opened our island steppingstone path straight across the mid-Pacific. Our Seabees couldn't dig a trench for a sewer pipe without digging up dead Japanese. But even so, the island was transformed, as we so rapidly transformed all our islands that were destroyed in the taking. It is a great air base now.

Naval officers met our plane despite the hour, loaded us into jeeps, and drove us a few hundred yards to a mess hall. A cool night breeze was blowing, and it seemed wonderful to be on the ground again, even such scant and sorrowful ground as this. For an hour we sat around a white-linened table, drinking coffee and sipping iced fruit juice. You would hardly have known you were not in America. And then we were off again, to fly through the sightless night, westward and on westward.

After we took off, our plane climbed noisily and laboriously for about half an hour, then it leveled off into steady and droning flight. Gradually the intense tropical heat of the ground faded away, and a chill came over the cabin.

The flight orderly turned on the heater, adjusting it until we were comfortable in our light clothes, even without jackets. We were not to stop again until we reached the Marianas.

Passengers were not allowed to smoke until the plane had stopped climbing and leveled off. Then the flight orderly stood at the head of the cabin and shouted in good Navy language, "The smoking lamp is lit," and brought around paper cups for ash trays. About every three hours he would wake us up to feed us – good food, too, and served on trays just as on the regular airlines. The way they poured food into us got to be a joke among the passengers. They fed us at every stop, and about every three hours in the air.

The flight orderly was a sailor who did the same job as a steward on the airlines. We had two crews and two flight orderlies during our long trip; our original crew stopped off halfway for a day's rest, and a new crew came on.

We were sixteen passengers – twelve Navy and Army officers (one a Marine Corps general), three enlisted men, and myself, the only civilian aboard. Both our flight orderlies were swell boys; they took good care of us, were friendly and willing, treated us all alike, and weren't a bit scared of the high rank aboard. They wore plain blue Navy dungarees and blue shins, and worked with their sleeves rolled up.

Our first one was Seaman Howard Liner, of Lubbock, Texas. He used to sell "Dr. Pepper" before he joined the Navy. Howard had made thirty-six trips across the Pacific, and enjoyed every one of them. He got back to San Francisco frequently, and on his next trip his wife was coming up from Lubbock to see him. Howard always had a little brown pencil stuck behind his ear.

The other flight orderly was Seaman Don Jacobi, of San Gabriel, California. He wore a plaited leather belt from which hung a big bunch of keys and a hunting knife in a scabbard. It was his seventh trip. He seemed quite mature, yet I found he was only eighteen and had quit high school to join the Navy. His one ambition was to finish school after the war, and go on to college.

It's mighty tiresome sitting in the same seat on an airplane for nearly twenty-four hours, even when the seats are reclining ones, as ours were. The worst part is trying to sleep; you doze for a while and then you start squirming, because you can't stretch your legs out and your knees start to hurt. Consequently those who have traveled a lot by air try to find someplace to lie down. The floor is good, but a stack of mail sacks is better. There was mail piled up in the rear four seats, so I took my blanket and started fixing myself up on the mail bags. An Army colonel said, "I just tried that, but had to give it up. There are too many square boxes inside the sacks and they stick into you." Rut being smaller than the colonel, I discovered I could sort of snake myself between the hard places in the sacks. And that way I slept most of the journey to the Marianas.

But there was one funny thing I'd never experienced before in flying. The plane had quite a bit of vibration, which would carry through my head if it touched the plane anywhere. That didn't bother me, but for some odd physiological reason the vibration made the tip of my nose itch so badly I had to scratch it all the lime. And so I dozed the night away, really only half asleep because of the constant necessity for scratching my nose.

Our chief pilot on the last long leg of our flight from Honolulu to the Marianas was Lieutenant Commander Don Skirvin. His family owns big hotels in Oklahoma City and even if you didn't know, you could tell from his creased hands and neck that he was either a Texan or an Oklahoman. Lieutenant Commander Skirvin had never worked at the hotel business, though. He had to have freedom to gad about the world. He had been flying eighteen years; he flew for oil companies in South America, and went to Spain during the revolution and flew combat there. Then came our war and he went into the Navy and was a combat flier in the South Pacific. But he liked big planes best, and was at that time transpacific skipper on those huge airliners.

Just before daylight Lieutenant Commander Skirvin sent the orderly back to wake me up and ask me to come forward to the pilot's compartment. He had me sit in the copilot's seat, and from that lofty vantage point on this monster of the air I saw the dawn gradually touch and lighten the cottony acres of clouds over the wide Pacific. Flying is mostly monotonous and dull, but there are always peaks of grandeur in every flight. Seeing that dawn come was one of them. It was an exaltation, and I couldn't help but be thrilled by it.. Lieutenant Commander Skirvin took movies as a hobby, and had shot 1,500 feet of color film of just such dawns and sunsets. Me said the folks at home wrote that if he saw such things often it was no wonder he liked to fly.

We came out of the boundless sky and over our island destination just a little after dawn. The island was green and beautiful – and terribly far from home. That we could have drawn ourselves to it so unerringly out of the vast Pacific spaces seemed incredible. It was like a blind man walking alone across a field, and putting his finger directly on some previously designated barb of a wire fence. But as I say, they do it all the time.

Lieutenant Commander Skirvin asked if I would like to stay up front while we landed. Indeed I would, for that is a rare invitation. I stood just behind the two pilots while we circled the field and dropped lower and circled again. Landing one of those immense planes is like a set of exercises in school. The copilot takes a printed list, encased in plexiglass, from the instrument board. Then he starts reading aloud, down the list. After each item the pilot calls back "check." It takes five minutes to go through all the complicated adjustments to change the plane from something that will fly to something that will merge successfully with the earth. Always the typed list is read aloud and checked to make sure that not a single thing is forgotten.

And then we were ready. It was hot down close to the ground, and sweat was pouring off us. Over his radio the copilot asked the ground for permission to land. Lieutenant Commander Skirvin twisted himself more firmly into his seat, took a heavy grip on the control wheel, pushed forward on the stick, and down we went.

When you fly, there is no sense of speed at all. It is as though you were sitting forever in one spot. But when you land, the earth comes up to you with appalling speed. Things go faster and faster. Everybody is tense. The whole field rushes toward you almost as in a nightmare. It is the most thrilling thing about flying. And then you blend into the earth. Those planes are so big and stand so high that it seemed to me we were still fifty feet in the air when we felt the wheels touch. The plane stuck to the runway and rushed on forward with shocking speed.

The runway was long, and Lieutenant Commander Skirvin called, "We'll use all of it, for I don't believe in tromping on the brakes." Gradually we slowed, and when we'd come almost to a stop a jeep pulled out in front of us. On the back of it was a big blackboard displaying the words "Follow me." The jeep slowly led us to our parking place. Then the copilot read off another list, while the pilot pulled levers and turned switches and called "check." It took more than a minute to transform that great metal bird from something miraculously animate into something that stood lifeless on the ground. And then the door opened and we stepped down onto the strange soil of the Marianas Islands – close at last to the vast sprawling war of the Pacific.

It was tropical there, wonderfully so. It looked tropical, and best of all, it felt tropical. We arrived in the good season, and it was like the pleasantest part of summer at home.

We got from the Navy a long-billed "baseball" cap to shield our eyes from the sun. In our clothes closet an electric light burned constantly keeping it dry so that our clothes wouldn't mildew. We changed our leather wrist-watch straps for canvas ones, since leather would mildew on our arm. We put on heavy high-topped shoes again, because it still rained some and the red mud was sloppy. And instead of the light socks you'd think we'd wear for coolness, we put on heavy ones to help cushion our feet in the big shoes, and to absorb the moisture. Officers wore their sun-glass cases hooked to their belts. Ties were unknown.

There was no glass in the windows. Wide slanting eaves jutted out far beyond the windows in all the permanent barracks buildings, for when it rains it really pours. And as someone said, it rains "horizontally." Since the rainy season was supposed to be over, every time it showered during the day the Californians in camp would point out that the weather was "unusual."

Lieutenant Commander Max Miller and I stayed in a room of a Bachelor Officers Quarters – or BOQ. Our famous Seabees have put them up all over the islands we took over from the Japanese. The quarters were in the curved form of immense Quonset huts, made of corrugated metal and with concrete floors. Some of them were even two-storied. Each had a wide hall down the center and individual rooms on each side. The walls were cream-colored; the outside one was almost all window to let in lots of air. The spaces were screened but not glassed, for it never gets so cold that anyone wants to shut the window. But it is pleasantly cool at night, and we slept under one blanket. Each room had a clothes closet, a washstand, and a chest of drawers. And also two beds. Those beds were the talk of the Marianas. They were American beds, with double mattresses, soft and wonderful. As everybody said, they were finer beds than you'd have at home. I ran into one Army officer who had served in Europe, and he laughed and said, "After the way we roughed it there, I feel self-conscious about sleeping like this over here. But if the Navy wants to send over these beds, I'm sure as hell going to sleep in them."

Naturally everybody on the islands didn't live like that: the quarters were only for transient visitors like myself, and staff officers. The great working camps of the Seabees and the troops were largely tents furnished with ordinary cots. But on the whole, the islands having been improved over several months, everybody lived pretty comfortably.

Max and I had a reception committee when we walked into our room. A half dozen Seabees wore throwing old lumber into a truck just outside our window. We hadn't been in the room two seconds when one Seabee called through the window: "Say, aren't you Ernie Pyle?" I said, "Right," and he said, "Whoever thought we'd meet you here? I recognized you from your picture." All the others stopped work and gathered outside the window while we talked through the screen. It made me fee! good all day, being welcomed like that during my first few minutes in the strange and faraway Marianas. The fellow who did the greeting was Seaman Peter Zelles, of 1117 Michigan Street, Toledo, Ohio.

The Navy furnished orderlies for these rooms, to keep them clean. Mostly they were colored boys, regular enlisted men. Pretty soon our orderly walked in, and he started staring at me and I at him, for he sure looked familiar. He was a great tall fellow, and he grinned and we shook hands. We had been on the same ship together when we invaded Sicily. He was a table waiter then; Elijah Scott, of 261 Garfield Street, Detroit, a steward's mate second class. He had been on the other side of the world nearly a year, spent eight months in America, and now there he was in the Pacific, almost as new an arrival as I.

And that wasn't all. Within another half hour there was a knock on the door and in walked an Army major with a big grin. "Well," he said, "I see you haven't got any fatter since the old days in Sicily and Italy." He was Major Pete Eldred, of Tucson, Arizona. He had been public relations officer for the Seventh Army ill Sicily. There he was a press censor in the middle of the Western Pacific, sitting on my bed talking about what used to be. Sometimes the world gets almost ridiculously small. I expected my father and Aunt Mary to climb through the window any minute.

CHAPTER TWO

Marianas Occupied

O NE thing that might help you grasp what life was like out here is
to realize that even a little island is lots bigger than you think.
Though many, many thousands of Americans lived in camps and at
airfields and in training centers and harbors over the islands occupied
by us, a man rarely knew many people outside his own special unit.
Even though the islands are small by our standards, they're big
enough; it would be as impossible for one man to see or know
everybody on any one of these islands as it would be to know everybody
in Indianapolis. You could live and work in your section and never visit
another section for weeks or months at a time.

For one thing, transportation was short. We were still building
furiously, such fast and fantastic building as you never dreamed of.
Everything that runs was being used, and there was little left over just
to run around in for fun. And anyhow there was no place to go. What
towns there were had been destroyed; there was nothing even
resembling a town or city on the islands. The natives had been set up
in improvised camps, but those offered no "city life" attractions.

Driving around one of the islands, we went through a town that had
been destroyed by bombing and shelling. It had been a good-sized place,
quite modern, too, in a tropical way, with a city plaza and municipal

buildings and paved streets. Many of the buildings were of stone or mortar. In destruction, it looked exactly the same as the ruined cities all over Europe look; the same jagged half-standing walls, the stacks of rubble, the empty houses you could see through, the roofless homes, the deep craters in the gardens. There was just one difference. Out here tropical vegetation is lush, and Nature thrusts up her greenery so swiftly through rubble of destruction that the ruins were now festooned with vines and green leaves, and it gave them a look of being very old and time-worn ruins instead of fresh and modern ones.

An American soldier in Europe, even though the towns may be "off limits" to him or destroyed completely, still had a sense of being near a civilization like his own. But out in the Pacific there was nothing like that. You were on an island, the natives were strange people, there was no city and no place to go. If you had a three-day pass you'd probably spend it lying on your cot. Eventually, boredom and the "island complex" started to take hold.

For that reason the diversions supplied by the Army were even more important in the Pacific than in Europe. Before I left America I heard that one island had more than 200 outdoor movies on it, and I thought whoever told that must be crazy, for in Europe the average soldier didn't very often get a chance to see a movie. But the guy wasn't crazy. The three Marianas Islands had a total of 233 outdoor movies on them, and they showed every night. Even if it wasn't a good movie, it killed the time between supper and bed. The theaters were usually on the slope of a hill, forming a natural amphitheater. The men sat on the ground, or brought their own boxes, or sometimes the ends of metal bomb crates were used for chairs. As you drove along, you'd sometimes pass three movies not more than 300 yards apart. That was mainly because there was not enough transportation to haul the men any distance, so the movie had to come to them.

There was a lot of other diversion provided besides movies. One island boasted 65 theater stages where soldiers themselves put on "live" shows, or where USO troupes performed. Forty pianos had been scattered around at these places. In Europe it was a lucky bunch of soldiers who got their hands on a radio. In these small Pacific islands, the Army distributed 3,500 radios, and a regular station was broadcasting all the time – music, news, shows.

The sports program was big; on one island alone there were 95 softball diamonds, 35 regular diamonds, 225 volleyball and 30 basketball courts, and 35 boxing arenas. Boxing was very popular. They had as high as 18,000 men watching a boxing match. In addition to these activities, which were planned and supervised, the boys did a lot to amuse themselves. The American is adept at fixing up any old place in the world to look like home, with little picket fences and all kinds of Rube Goldberg contraptions inside to make it more livable. And this uses up time. For example, the coral sea bottom inside the reef around these islands abounds with fantastic miniature marine life, weird and colorful. Soldiers made glass-bottomed boxes for themselves, and waded out to look at the beautiful sea bottom. I've seen them out there like that for hours, just staring down at the sea bottom. At home they wouldn't have gone to an aquarium if you'd built one in their back yard.

You may wonder why we had any American troops at all there in the Marianas Islands, since they are 1,500 miles away from the Philippines, China, or Japan itself. Well, it's because in this Pacific war of vast water distances, we had to make gigantic bases of each group of islands taken, in order to build up supplies and preparations for future invasions farther on. The Marianas happen to be a sort of crossroads in the Western Pacific. Stuff can go either west or north from there. Whoever sits in the Marianas can have his finger on the whole wide ebb of a Pacific war. Our naval and military leaders made no bones about it, for the Japs knew it anyhow, but they were too far away to do anything about it.

Scores of thousands of troops of all kinds were there. Furious building was going on. Planes arrived on schedule from all directions as though it were Chicago Airport – coming from thousands of miles over water. Convoys unloaded unbelievable tonnages. These islands were humming throughout the war and they will never return to their former placid life, for we were building on almost every inch of usable land. Supplies in staggering quantities were being stacked up there for future use. You could take your pick of K rations or lumber or bombs, and you'd find enough there to feed a city, build one, or blow it up. Fleets based there between engagements. Combat troops came there to train; other troops came back to rest. Great hospitals were set up for our wounded. Pipelines crisscrossed the islands. Trucks bumper to bumper dashed forward as though they were on the Western Front. Oxcart trails turned almost overnight into four-lane macadam highways for military traffic.

There was no blackout in the islands. If raiders came the lights were turned off, but they seldom came any more. The Marianas were pretty safe. Great long macadam airstrips were in operation and others were being laid. The Marianas were the base for some of our B-29 bomber fleets, and it was growing and growing and growing. Thousands of square tents, thousands of curved steel Quonset huts, thousands of huge, permanent warehouses and office buildings dotted the islands. Lights burned all night and the roar of planes, the clank of bulldozers and the clatter of hammers were constant. A strange contrast to the stillness that dwelt amidst that greenery for so many centuries.

There are fifteen islands in the chain, running due north and south. They string out a total distance of more than 400 miles. We were on the southern end. We held only three islands, but they are the biggest and the only three that count. The other islands were completely "neutralized" by our occupancy of these three. There were a few Japs living on some of the others, but there was nothing they could do to harm us; most of them had no inhabitants at all. The islands we took in the summer of 1944 were Guam, Tinian, and Saipan. Guam had been ours for many years before Japan took it away from us just after Pearl Harbor. Tinian and Saipan had been Japanese since the last war.

Guam is the biggest, and southernmost. Tinian and Saipan are right together, 120 miles north of Guam. You can fly up there in less than an hour, and our transport planes shuttled back and forth several times daily on regular schedule. They had to make a "dog-leg" around the island of Rota, about halfway up, for there were still Japs there with 50-caliber machine guns, and they'd shoot.

I went to all three of our islands, and I must admit two things – that I liked it there, and that I was thrilled by what the Americans were doing. And from all I picked up, I think it can be said that most

Americans liked the Marianas Islands, assuming they had to be away from home at all. The savage heat and the dread diseases and the awful jungles of the more southern Pacific islands do not exist there. The climate is good, the islands are pretty, and the native Chamorros are nice people. Health conditions among our men were excellent. The mosquito and fly problem had been licked. There was almost no venereal disease. Food was good. The weather was always warm but not cruelly hot and almost always a breeze was blowing.

Yes, the islands are a paradise and life there is fine – except that it's empty and the monotony eventually gnaws at a man.

One day, I finally got around to a month-overdue haircut. My barber was a soldier, working in a tent, and I sat in an old-fashioned black leather Japanese barber chair he had dug up on the island. He had been trained in the conversational school of bartering, and as the snipped gray locks fell about my shoulders, there came forth from him such a tale of cruel woe and unkind fate as I had never heard in this world. He was Pfc. Eades Thomas, from Richmond, Kentucky, near Lexington in the horse country. In fact Thomas was a horse trainer before the war, and never a barber at all. He just picked that up on the run somewhere. Well, Thomas had been in the Pacific thirty-three months. When it began to look as though he might as well count on settling down for life, he had married a Scottish girl some months back in Honolulu. Shortly after that he was shipped on out here, and he hadn't seen her since.

The morning of the day I sat in Thomas's barber chair the Army was sending a few Japanese prisoners back to Hawaii by airplane and they had to have guards for them. One of Thomas's officers told him he would put him down for the trip so that he could get a couple of days in Hawaii to see his wife. The officer meant to keep his word, but he had a bad memory for names. When he went to write down Thomas's name for the trip, he wrote another guy's name, thinking it was Thomas. By the time Thomas found it out, it was too late. "I could have cried," he said. And I could have too. I felt so terrible about it I couldn't get it off my mind, and was talking about it to an officer that evening.

"Oh," he said. "I happen to know about that. I'll go and tell Thomas right away and he won't feel so bad. We got orders not to send the prisoners after all, so the whole thing was called off. Nobody went."

Which is the kind of joy you get when you stop hitting yourself on the head with the hammer, but at least it's better than if you kept on hitting it.

On that same island I ran into a couple of old Hoosier boys, who had followed in my inglorious footsteps at Indiana University. One was Lieutenant Ed Rose, who was editor of the *Daily Student* in 1938, just as I was for a while in 1922. Apparently it doesn't make any difference what year you were editor of the *Student*, you still wind up in the Marianas Islands. The other was Lieutenant Bill Morris, from Anderson, Indiana, who graduated from our illustrious Alma Mater in 1942. Both the boys were mail censors out here. Life was kind enough to them, and they didn't have much to kick about.

Just as I was leaving, they came and thrust a package into my hands, and said would I accept a little gift from the two of them? It was a. dark poisonous liquid with which you're probably not familiar, but one much sought after out here. A fellow does feel like a heel accepting bountiful gifts from strangers. But I figured I'd been a heel for a long time and it was too late to reform then, so I grabbed the gift and fled before they could change their l minds. Thanks again, boys.

In the Pacific the marines have an expression all their own for the Japs. They called them "Japes," which is a combination of "Jap" and "ape." Then the fliers were taking it up, and there were various versions of it. I noticed a lot of people unconsciously pronouncing Japan as "Jay-pan," just as in Africa we always used to say "A-rab" instead of "errab," as we were taught in school. Sometimes they carried it into multi-syllables, such as "We're going to Jay-pan-man-land tomorrow."

Another slang word is "gear," which apparently means a bigshot. For example: Every afternoon a soldier brought about fifty letters written by enlisted men into our hut for the officers to censor. The officers in the hut had a habit of doing the letters right off to get it over with. They took about six apiece, and everybody had finished in a few minutes.

The boy who brought the letters around was a Spaniard – Gustavo Gonzalez, of 2620 Avenue K, Galveston, Texas. He talked with an accent and was quite a character. The fliers enjoyed kidding back and forth with him. When Gonzalez came back for the letters, they were all ready. Apparently the other huts didn't do so well by him, and he had to wait. For as he left he turned at the door and said to the officers: "You guys are all right. If I was a gear I'd promote you all."

There were still Japs on the three islands of the Marianas chain that we had occupied for more than six months. The estimate ran into several hundred. They hid in the hills and in caves, and came out at night to forage for food. Actually many of their caves were so well stocked that they could go for months without getting too hungry. Our men didn't do anything about the Japs any more. Oh, troops in training for combat would go out on a Jap hunt now and then just for practice and bring in a few. But they were no menace to us, and by and large we just ignored them. A half dozen or so gave up every day.

The Japs didn't try to practice any sabotage on our stuff. It would take another Jap to figure out why. The Japanese were thoroughly inconsistent in what they did, and very often illogical. They did the silliest things. Here are a few examples. One night some of our Seabees left a bulldozer and an earth mover sitting alongside the road up in the hills. During the night, the Japs came down. They couldn't hurt anybody, but they could have put that machinery out of commission for a while. Even with only a rock they could have smashed the spark plugs and ruined the carburetor. They didn't do any of those things. They merely spent the night cutting palm fronds off nearby trees and laying them over the big machinery. Next morning when the Seabees arrived they found their precious equipment completely "hidden."

On another island, there were many acts of sabotage the Japs could have committed. But all they ever did was to come down at night and move the wooden stakes the engineers had lined up for the next day's construction of buildings!

There is another story of a Jap who didn't take to the hills like the rest, but who stayed for weeks right in the most thickly American-populated section of the island, right down by the seashore. He hid in the bushes just a few feet from a path where hundreds of Americans walked daily. They found out later that he even used the officers' outdoor shower bath after they got through, and raided their kitchens at night. There was a Jap prison enclosure nearby and for weeks, peering out of the bushes, he studied the treatment his fellow soldiers were getting, watched how they ate, watched to see if they were dwindling away from malnutrition. And then one day he came out and gave himself up. He said he had convinced himself they were being treated all right, so he was ready to surrender.

And here's another one. An American officer was idly sitting on an outdoor box toilet one evening after work, philosophically studying the ground, as men will do. Suddenly he was startled. Startled is a mild word for it. For there he was, caught with his pants down, so to speak, and in front of him stood a Jap with a rifle. But before anything could happen the Jap laid the rifle on the ground in front of him, and began salaaming up and down like a worshiper before an idol. The Jap later said that he had been hunting for weeks for somebody without a rifle to give himself up to, and had finally figured out that the surest way to find an unarmed prospective captor was to catch one on the toilet!

But don't let these little stories mislead you into thinking the Japs were easy, after all. For they were a very nasty people while the shootin' was going on.

Soldiers and marines told me stories by the dozen about how tough the Japs were, yet how dumb too; how illogical, yet how uncannily smart at times; how easy to rout when disorganized, yet how brave. I became more confused with each story. At the end of one evening I said, "I can't make head or tail out of what you've told me. I'm trying to learn about the Jap soldiers, but everything you say about them seems to be inconsistent."

"That's the answer," my friends said. "They are inconsistent. They do the damnedest things. But they're dangerous fighters just the same."

They told one story about a Jap officer and six men who were surrounded on a beach by a small bunch of marines. As the marines approached, they could see the Jap giving emphatic orders to his men, and then all six bent over and the officer went along the line and chopped off their heads with his sword. As the marines closed in, he stood knee-deep in the surf and beat his bloody sword against the water in a fierce gesture of defiance, just before they shot him. What code led the officer to kill his own men rather than let them fight to the death is again something only another Jap would know.

Another little story. A marine sentry walking up and down before a command post on top of a steep bluff one night heard a noise in the brush on the hillside below. He called a couple of times, got no answer, then fired an exploratory shot down into the darkness. In a moment there was a loud explosion from below. A solitary Jap hiding down there had put a hand grenade to his chest. Why he did that, instead of tossing it up over the bluff and getting himself a half dozen Americans, is beyond an American's comprehension.

On Saipan, they told of a Jap plane that appeared overhead one bright noonday, all alone. He obviously wasn't a photographic plane, and they couldn't figure out what he was doing. Then something came out of the plane, and fluttered down. It was a little paper wreath, with a long streamer to it. He had flown it all the way from Japan, and dropped it "In Honor of Japan's Glorious Dead" on Saipan. We shot him down into the sea a few minutes later, as he undoubtedly knew we would before he ever left Japan. The gesture was touching – but so what?

As I talked with marines, I began to get over that creepy feeling that fighting Japs was like fighting snakes or ghosts. They were indeed queer, but they were people with certain tactics and now by much experience our men had learned how to fight them. As far as I could sec, our men were no more afraid of the Japs than they were of the Germans. They were afraid of them as any modern soldier is afraid of his foe, not because they are slippery or ratlike, but simply because they have weapons and fire them like good tough soldiers. And the Japs were human enough to be afraid of us in exactly the same way.

CHAPTER THREE

The B-29s

BEFORE starting out on my long tours with the Navy, I decided to visit the famous B-29 Superfortress boys who were bombing Japan from the Marianas. I had "kinfolk" flying on the B-29s, and I thought I'd kill two birds, visiting and writing at the same time. So there I was sitting on a screened porch in my underwear, comfortable as a cat, with the surf beating on the shore and a lot of bomber pilots swimming out front. The B-29 boy$» from commandant down to enlisted men of lowest rank, lived well. They were all appreciative of their good fortune. Of course, they all would rather have been home, but who wouldn't?

The man I went to visit was Lieutenant Jack Bales, another farm boy from near Dana, Indiana. Jack is a sort of nephew of mine. He isn't exactly a nephew, but it's too complicated to explain; I used to hold him on my knee and all that sort of tiling. But now he was twenty-six, and starting to get bald like his "uncle." Jack's folks still live just a mile down the road from our farm. Jack left the farm and went to the University of Illinois and got a good education. He was just ready to become a famous lawyer when the war came along and he enlisted. He spent a year as a private, then got a commission and flew over from Nebraska with the B-29s in October of 1944.

When I telephoned Jack and said I'd be out in about an hour to stay a few days, he said he would put up an extra cot in his hut for me. When I got there the cot was up, with blankets and mattress covers laid out on it. Jack had told the boys he was having a visitor, and on the assumption it was a woman six eager volunteers had been helping him put up the cot. When I showed up, skinny and bald, it was an awful letdown, but they were all decent about it.

Jack lived in a steel Quonset hut with ten other fliers. Most of them were pilots, but Jack was a radioman; he and another fellow had charge of all his squadron's radio. He didn't have to go on missions except now and then to check up. But I learned, to my astonishment and pride, that he had been on more missions than anybody else in his squadron. In fact, he had been on so many that his squadron commander had forbidden him to go for a while. Not that he enjoyed it; nobody but a freak likes to go on combat missions. He went because he had things to learn, and because he could contribute something by being there. But he seemed to show no strain from the ordeal; he said that sitting around camp got so monotonous he sort of welcomed a mission just for a change. Another time or two and he would have his quota authorizing him to go back to rest camp for a while.

During flight Jack sat in a little compartment in the rear of the plane, unable to see out. In all his missions over Japan he had seen only one Jap fighter. Not that they didn't have plenty around, but he was so busy he seldom got to a window for a peek. The one time he did, a Jap came slamming under the plane so close it almost took the skin off.

Like all combat crewmen, Jack spent all night and at least half of each day lying on his cot. He held the record in his hut for "sack time," which means just lying on a cot doing nothing. He had his work so organized that it didn't take much of his time between missions, and since there's nothing else to do, you just lie around. Jack said he had got so lazy he wouldn't be able to face a job after the war, so he thought he'd work into civilian life gradually by going back to school again.

The B-29 fliers slept on folding canvas cots, with rough white sheets. Sleeping is wonderful in the islands, and along toward morning you usually pull a blanket over you. Each flier had a dresser of wooden shelves he'd made for himself, and there were several homemade tables scattered around. The walls were plastered with maps, snapshots, and pin-up girls – but I noticed that real pin-up girls (wives and mothers) dominated the movie beauties. Eight of the ten men in the hut were married.

Although the food was good, most of the boys got packages from home. One kid wrote and told his folks to slow up a little, that he was snowed under with packages. Jack had had two jars of Indiana fried chicken from my Aunt Mary. She cans it and seals it in Mason jars, and it's wonderful. She sent me some in France, but I'd left before it got there. Jack took some of his fried chicken in his lunch over Tokyo one day. We Hoosiers sure do get around, even the chickens.

When a headline said "Superforts Blast Japan Again," it didn't mean that Japan was being blown sky high and that she'd be bombed out of the war within a week or two.

That wasn't the case. We were at the time just starting on a long and tough program of bombing and even with heavy and constant attacks it was going to take years to reduce Japan by bombing alone. And our bombings then were not yet heavy. Too, we had lots of things to contend with: distance was the main thing; Jap fighters and ack-ack and foul weather were other things. The weather over Japan was the enemy's best defense. As one pilot jokingly suggested, "The Nips should broadcast the weather to us every night, and save us both lots of trouble."

Almost the first thing the B-29 boys asked me was, "Do the people at home think the B-29s are going to win the war?" I told them the papers played up the raids, and that many wishful-thinking people felt the bombings might turn the trick. And the boys said: "That's what we were afraid of. Naturally we want what credit we deserve, but our raids certainly aren't going to win the war."

The B-29 raids were important, just as every island taken and every ship sunk was important. But it would be all out of proportion to say they were a dominant factor in our Pacific war. I say this not to belittle the B-29 boys because they were wonderful. I say it because they themselves wanted it understood by the folks at home.

Their lots was a tough one. The worst part was that they were over water every inch of the way to Japan and every inch of the way back. And, brother, it's a lot of water. The average time for one of their missions was more than fourteen hours. The flak and fighters over Japan were bad enough, but that tense period was fairly short. They were over the empire for only twenty minutes to an hour, depending on their target, and Jap fighters followed them for about fifteen minutes off the coast. What gave the boys the willies was "sweating out" those six or seven hours of ocean beneath them on the way back. To make it worse, it was usually at night. Some of the planes were bound to be shot up, and just staggering along. There was always the danger of running out of gas, because of many forms of overconsumption. If you had one engine gone, the others were liable to quit. If anything happened, you went into the ocean; that is known as ditching. Around a B-29 base you heard the word "ditching" almost more than any other. Ditching in the Pacific wasn't like ditching in the English Channel where your chances of being picked up were awfully good. Out here it was usually fatal. A search and rescue system had been set up but it's mighty hard to find a couple of little rubber boats in a big, big ocean. The fact that we did rescue about a fifth of our ditched fliers is amazing to me. Yes, that long drag back home after the bombing was a definite mental hazard, and it was what eventually made the boys sit and stare.

Maybe you've heard of the "buddy system" in the infantry. They used it in the B-29s, too. For instance, if a plane was in distress on the way back and had to fall behind, somebody dropped back with him to keep him company. They've known planes to come clear home accompanied by a "buddy," and you could truthfully say that some might not have made it except for the extra courage given them by having company. But the important thing about the buddy system was that if a plane did have to ditch, the buddy could fix his exact position and get surface rescuers on the way.

One morning after a mission, my friend Major Gerald Robinson was lying on his cot resting and reminiscing, and he said, "You feel so damn helpless when the others get in trouble. The air will be full of radio calls from those guys saying they've only got two engines or they're running short on gas. I've been lucky and there I'll be sitting with four engines and a thousand extra gallons of gas. I could spare any of them one engine and five hundred gallons of gas if I could just get it to them. It makes you feel so damn helpless."

My nephew's B-29 squadron was commanded by Lieutenant Colonel John H. Griffith, of Plymouth, Pennsylvania. He walked into our Quonset hut the first night I was there and grinned sort of knowing-like as we were introduced. I felt our paths had crossed somewhere in the dim past, but I couldn't recall it. Finally he said, "Remember the *Rangitiki?*"

"Oh, for God's sake, of course," I said. The *Rangitiki* was the ship that took us from England to Africa in the fall of 1942. Colonel Griffith was in a nearby cabin on that trip and we became well acquainted. But the war is big and time flies, and you do forget.

Colonel Griffith flew combat missions out of both England and Africa. And now on this side of the world he had made eleven missions to Japan. But from then on, being an executive, he was being restricted to four missions a month. Once on a mission the bombardier had his leg blown almost off. As Colonel Griffith was dragging him back into the pilot's compartment, he thoughtlessly took off his own oxygen mask. In a moment he passed out and fell over. But freakishly he fell with his face right in the mask, and was revived.

Although still young, Colonel Griffith had been in the Army eight years, and planned to stay in after the war. His wife and baby and dog were waiting for him at Lagrange Park, Illinois.

The colonel had been living with the pilots in the Quonset hut, but a few days before I arrived they finished his new house. You should have seen it. It was a skeleton framework of two-by-fours about thirty feet square, roofed with canvas and walled only with screen wire, tropical fashion. The roof had an overhang about six feet wide all around to keep out the rain. Inside, they'd given it the semblance of a many-roomed house by putting up little hip-high partitions of brown burlap. It made it seem like a living room, bedroom, bath, kitchen, and sun porch, although it was actually just one big room. The place was wonderfully comfortable. It had four desks, two cots and ten chairs, and yet there was lots of room left over. There were an icebox, a radio, and a field telephone; a big clothes closet and a washbowl and shower, the water supplied from two 50-gallon barrels up the hillside. Incidentally, Colonel Griffith still had the same alarm clock he took with him when he went to England nearly three years ago.

The wooden floor was painted battleship gray. Colonel Griffith liked to keep his floor clean, and he had a big sign on his screen door: "Please Remove Shoes Before Entering." He wasn't joking either. He even made his own commanding officer take off his shoes when he came to visit. He furnished his guests extra socks in case their feet got cold, which of course they didn't.

The house was built on stilts, amidst laurel and other wild, green shrubbery, only fifty feet from the sea. You came to it down the slope over a path cut out of the laurel, and once in the house you were utterly away from everything. Before you were only the curve of the lagoon, and the incessant pounding of rollers on the reef a hundred yards out, and the white clouds in the far blue sky. Several times a day sudden tropical showers drenched and cooled the place. If you had this house in America, it would cost $200 a month rent, yet the whole thing was built of packing boxes and metal bomb crates and Army leftovers.

It was on Colonel Griffith's porch that I wrote my dispatches. The only excuse for their not being better was that I couldn't seem to keep away from a low deck chair at the far end of the porch. And also I kept looking up the path to see if Sadie Thompson wasn't strolling down with her umbrella.

The B-29 is unquestionably a wonderful airplane. Outside of the famous old Douglas DC-3 workhorse, I've never heard of an airplane so unanimously praised by pilots. I took my first ride not long after I arrived in the Marianas. No, I didn't go on a mission to Japan; I don't believe in people going on missions unless they have to, and the pilots all agreed with me. But I went along on a little practice bombing trip of an hour and a half. The pilot was Major Gerald Robinson, who lived in our hut. His wife, incidentally, lived at 123 South Girard Street, Albuquerque, New Mexico, on the very same street with our white house.

I sat on a box between the pilots, both on the takeoff and for the landing, and much as I'd flown before, that was a real thrill. The islands are all relatively small, and you're no sooner off the ground than you're out over water, which feels funny. If the air is a little rough, sitting way up there in the nose is a very odd sensation, for the B-29 is so big that, instead of bumping or dropping, the nose goes into a willowy motion. It's rather like sitting out on the end of a green limb when it's swaying around.

The B-29 carries a crew of eleven. Some of them sit up in the cockpit and in the compartment just behind it. Some others sit in a compartment near the tail. The tail gunner sits all by himself, way back in the lonely tail turret. The body of the B-29 is so taken up with gas tanks and bomb racks that there was no way to get from front to rear compartments, so the manufacturers built a tunnel in the plane, right along the rooftop. The tunnel is round, just big enough to crawl in on your hands and knees, and is padded with blue cloth. It's more than thirty feet long, and the crew members crawled back and forth through it all the time. Major Russ Cheever reported that he accomplished the impossible one day by turning around in the tunnel.

On missions, some of the crew got into this tunnel and slept for an hour or so. But a lot of them couldn't do that; they said they got claustrophobia. There used to be some sleeping bunks on the B-29, but they'd been taken out, and there was hardly room even to lie down on the floor. A fellow does get sleepy on a fourteen-hour mission, and most of the pilots took naps in their seats. One pilot I know turned the plane over to his copilot, went back to the tunnel for "a little nap," and didn't return for six hours, just before they hit the coast of Japan.

The B-29 is a very stable plane and hardly anybody ever got sick even in rough weather. The boys smoked in the plane, and the mess hall gave them a small lunch of sandwiches and oranges and cookies to eat on the way. On mission days all flying crewmen, even those not going on the mission, got all the fried eggs they wanted for breakfast. That was the only day they had eggs.

The crewmen wore their regular clothes on missions, usually coveralls. They didn't have to wear heavy fleece-lined clothes and all such bulky gear, because the cabin was heated. But they did slip on heavy steel flak vests as they approached the target. They didn't wear oxygen masks except when over the target, because the cabin was sealed and "pressurized" – simulating a constant altitude of 8,000 feet. Once in a great while one of the plexiglass "blisters" where the gunners sit blew out from the strong pressure inside, and then everybody had to grab his oxygen mask in a big hurry. The crew always wore oxygen masks over the target, for a shell through the plane "depressurized" the cabin instantly, and everybody would pass out.

The boys spoke frequently of the unbelievably strong winds encountered at high altitudes over Japan. It was nothing unusual to hit a 150-mi lean-hour wind, and my nephew said that one day his plane ran into one of 250 miles an hour.

Another thing that often puzzled and amused the boys was picking up news on their radios, when only halfway home, that their bombing mission had been announced in Washington. All the world knew about it, but they still had a thousand miles of ocean to cross before it was finished.

I've always felt the great 500-mile auto race at Indianapolis was the most exciting event – in terms of human suspense – that I've ever known. The start of a B-29 mission to Tokyo, from the spectator's standpoint, was almost the same as the Indianapolis race.

On mission day people were out early to see the start. Soldiers sat in groups on favorite high spots around the field – on tops of buildings, on tops of bulldozers along the runway, on mounds that gave a better view – and a few bold souls even stood at the very end of the runway to snap amateur pictures as the thundering planes passed just over their heads. As the planes taxied out, it was just like the cars at Indianapolis leaving their pits to line up for the start. You waved farewell to your own special friends, and then got as fast as you could to your own favorite spot to watch the spectacle.

My nephew Jack wasn't on the first mission I saw start, off, so we drove in a jeep to the far end of the runway, and parked on a raised place alongside it, at a point where the planes had to be in the air – or else. "If a plane starts wheeling off the runway," Jack said, "we gotta run like hell." Most of the planes would be in the air long before they reached us. But a few either had trouble getting off or else their pilots were holding them down, for they just barely lifted in the last few feet of runway, and the amateur photographers hit the dirt so hard we had to laugh.

The spacing between them was perfect; there was never a blank spot, never a delay. When we turned from seeing one safely off the ground, there would be the next one coming down the runway. Any plane taking off was out over the water within a few seconds. It gave you goose flesh to see a plane clear the bluff by a mere few feet, then sink out of sight toward the water; that was because the pilots nosed down a little to get more flying speed. Pretty soon you'd see them come up into sight again.

That day there were no accidents at the start, but not all the planes got off. Two were canceled on the ground before starting, two ran halfway down the airstrip, then cut the power and came rolling off to the side, just like burned-out racing cars. One of them had locked brakes and was barely able to pull itself off the airstrip and out of the way. He stayed there alongside the runway as all the others roared past him, seeming, from our position, almost to lock wings with him as they passed. Finally they were all in the air, formed into flights, and vanishing into the sky from which some would never return. Just as at Indianapolis, there were a number of cars and men, and some of them you knew. They had trained for weeks for this day. At last the time had come, and in a few hours of desperate living everything would be changed. Some would be glorious in victory, some would be defeated in failure, some would be also-rans, and some – very probably – would be dead. That's the way I felt when the B-29s started out. It was just up to fate. In fifteen hours they would be back – those who were coming back. But there was no knowing ahead of time who it would be.

No sooner had the formations disappeared to the north on their long flight to Japan than single planes began coming back in. These are called "aborts," which is short for "abortives." It was a much-used word around a bomber base, and it meant the planes that had something happen to them that forbade their continuing on the long dangerous trip. Sometimes it happened immediately after takeoff; sometimes it didn't happen until they were almost there. The "aborts" came straggling back all day, hours apart.

The first abort that day had a bomb-bay door come open, and it wouldn't close. The second had part of the cowl flap come unfastened, and a mechanic undoubtedly caught hell for that. A third had a prop run away when he lost an engine. My friend Major Walter Todd, of Ogden, Utah, aborted. He blew a cylinder head clear off. He was within sight of Japan when it happened, and he beat the others back home by only half an hour. He flew thirteen and a half hours that day, and didn't even get credit for a mission. That's the way it goes.

Those left on the field idly looked at their watches as the long day wore on, mentally clocking the progress of their comrades. "They're about sighting the mainland now," you'd hear somebody say.

"They should be over the target by now. I'll bet they're catching hell," came a little later from somebody else.

By late afternoon you knew that by now, for good or bad, it was over with. We knew they were far enough off the coast so that the last Jap fighter had turned for home, leaving them alone with the night and their troubles and the long distance to come. Our planes bombed in formation, and stuck together until they'd left the Japanese coast, then they broke up and each man came home on his own. It was almost spooky the way they flew alone through the dark night for more than six hours, and all arrived at the little islands almost within a few minutes of each other.

Radio messages had been coming in since late afternoon. A flight leader would radio how the weather was, and report if anybody went down over the target. It wasn't a complete picture, but the reports were patched together to give a general idea of what had happened.

We lost planes that day. Some went down over the target. Some just disappeared, and the other boys never knew where they went. Some fought as long as they could to keep damaged planes going, then had to ditch into the ocean.

One tenacious planeload got back miraculously – it wasn't in the cards for them at all. They had been hit over the target, had to drop down and back alone, and the Jap fighters went for them, as they do for any cripple. Five fighters just butchered the plane, and there was nothing our boys could do about it. Yet they kept coming – how, nobody knows. Two of the crew were badly wounded. The horizontal stabilizers were shot away. The plane was riddled with holes. The pilot could keep control only by using the motors. Every half hour or so he would radio his fellow planes, "Am in right spiral and going out of control." But he would get control again, fly for an hour or so, and then radio once more that he was spiraling out of control. But somehow he made it home, and had to land without controls. Though he did wonderfully well, ho didn't quite pull it off. The plane hit at the end of the runway, and the engines came hurtling out, on fire. The wings flew off and the great fuselage broke in two and went careening across the ground. Yet every man came out of it alive, even the wounded ones.

Two other crippled planes cracked up on landing. It was not until late at night that the final tally was made, of known lost, and of missing. But hardly was the last returning bomber down when a lone plane took off into the night and headed northward, to be in the area by dawn where the ditchings were reported. And the others, after their excited stories were told, fell wearily into bed.

There are five officers and six enlisted men on the crew of a B-29. All the enlisted men of a crew stayed in the same hut, because that's the way the boys wanted it. Thus there were usually three crews of six men each in a Quonset hut. The enlisted men's huts were more crowded than the officers' but outside of that there was no difference. They had a few more duties than the officers when not on missions, but they still had plenty of spare time.

"My" crew was a grand bunch of boys, as I suppose most of them were. They had trouble sleeping the night before a mission, and they were tense before the takeoff. As one of them said at the plane just before leaving one morning, "How do you get rid of that empty feeling in your chest?" But they relaxed and expanded and practically floated away with good feeling once they got back with another one safe under their belts. The six enlisted men of my crew were Sergeants Joe Corcoran, of Woodhaven, Long Island, Fauad Smith, of Des Moines, New Mexico (near Raton), Joe McQuade, of Gallup, New Mexico, John Devaney, of 333 West Second Avenue, Columbus, Ohio, Norbert

Springman, of Wilmont, Minnesota, and Eugene Florio, of 1343 South California Boulevard, Chicago. Springman and Florio were radiomen, and all the others were gunners.

Sergeant Corcoran was the oldest of the crew. The first time I walked into their hut he called from his cot, "Hi, Ernie, the last time I saw you was in the Stork Club."

"But I've never been in the Stork Club in my life," I said.

So we puzzled over that awhile, and finally decided it must have been two other guys, or else I'd been living a double life I didn't know about. Sergeant Corcoran was a chiropractor before the war, and gave the boys free treatments. He practiced for three years at Jamaica, Long Island, and had a fine business worked up. I asked him how a chiropractor ever wound up to be a side gunner on a B-29, and he said damned if he knew.

It was unusual to find two men from thinly populated New Mexico on the same crew. Smith and McQuade never knew each other until they met there, and then they found out that they had joined the Anny the very same day. They were great buddies. McQuade was a fireman on the Santa Fe, and Smith had owned a grocery store, but finally had to sell it. They'd just had letters saying it was below zero back home, and they were at least thankful to be away from that.

Both the boys had had experiences. McQuade had made two trips to the Aleutians as a gunner on a ship, and Smith was then serving his second tour of aerial combat overseas. He had been in the South Pacific in the early days, and had flown fifty-three missions as gunner on B-17s. He had all his missions recorded on the back of his leather flying jacket – yellow bombs for the South Pacific, and red ones for Japan. He said he had room for only twenty-seven more missions on his jacket, and then he'd just have to quit. I asked Sergeant Smith if he hated to come back overseas as badly as I did.

"Twice as bad," he said.

"You couldn't."

"Well, as bad then," he said. "But I haven't griped so much about it since we got here. It's not near as bad as I expected. In fact we're living as good here as we did in America."

Sergeant Smith's odd first name – Fauad – is Syrian. He was

growing a funny little rectangular goatee, black as coal, and I asked him how long he was going to keep it He said, "Probably only until the colonel happens to notice it."

We were all gathered around Corcoran and Smith's cots one day when Corky reached under his cot and pulled out a huge rattrap to show me. It seems they had a mouse in the hut, who ate their candy and soap and was a general nuisance. They couldn't find a mousetrap, so they set this big rattrap. Every night Mr. Mouse ate all the cheese, even licked the plunger clean, but the trap was so strong it wouldn't go off. So finally Corcoran had strung thread through the cheese, hoping the mouse would get his teeth caught in it and thus yank the trap off.

Major Robinson, the airplane commander of the crew, had led his boys through almost two years of training before they came overseas. "That means a lot to have been together so long, doesn't it?" I asked.

"It means everything," one of the sergeants said. "We're a team."

The crew had been lucky. They were intact except for the bombardier who had had his leg almost blown off and was then back in Hawaii in a hospital. The enlisted men asked especially that I put the bombardier down as still part of the crew, even though he wasn't there any more. They'd been together so long, and they liked him so much. He was Lieutenant Paul O'Brien, of Dayton, Ohio.

My crew had a superstition, or maybe it was just a tradition. They all wore the same kind of cap when they started on a mission. It was a dark-blue baseball cap with the yellow numbers "80" on the crown. They had got the caps a couple of years before in Minneapolis when they were there on a weekend trip because of winning some kind of merit prize. The "80" was their unit number then, and although it had long since ceased to exist, they insisted on keeping it. Once in a while Major Robinson used to forget his cap, and the enlisted men would send somebody back after it before the mission started. But they had lost two of the caps. One was Lieutenant O'Brien's; he took it with him when he was evacuated. The other was Major Robinson's. His cap got so bloody from Lieutenant O'Brien's wound that he had to throw it away.

My crew lost their first plane right on the field when a Jap bomb got it. It was named "Battlin' Betty" after Major Robinson's wife, so he changed the name of his next ship from "Small Fry" to "Battlin' Betty II."

As I said before. Major Robinson carried a movie camera with him on every mission. One night when he came into the hut after a fourteen-hour mission over Tokyo, he held up his movie camera for me to see, and said, "Now I'm satisfied to quit. I got the picture today that should end it. There was a Jap fighter diving at the squadron ahead of us. He apparently didn't sec us at all, for he pulled up and turned his belly to us and just hung there, wide open. Every gun in our squadron let him have it. He just blew all to pieces. And I got the whole thing. So now I'm ready to lay it aside." He couldn't have the pictures developed till he got home, but sealed the film up in moisture-proof cloth against the tropical climate.

One of the most vital members of a bomber's family is the ground crew chief, even though he doesn't fly. He's the guy who sees that the airplane does fly. A good crew chief is worth his weight in gold. Major Robinson said he had the finest crew chief in the Marianas and I could believe it after seeing him. He was Sergeant Jack Orr, of $737 Normandy Street, Dallas, Texas. He was a married man, tall, good-looking and modest – and so conscientious it hurt. He took a mission harder than the flying crew members themselves.

Major Robinson said that on one trip they had had trouble and were the last ones in, long after the others had landed. Sergeant Orr was waiting for them at the "hard-stand." When they got out of the plane he was all over them, jumping up and down like a puppy dog, shouting and hugging them, and they could hardly quiet him down, he was so happy. Major Robinson said he was sort of embarrassed, but I heard him tell the story two or three times, so I know how touched he was. There is indeed a fraternalism in war that is hard for people at home to realize.

The funniest man in our hut of B-29 pilots was Captain Bill Gifford, of Buford, South Carolina. He was a lean, profane, and witty guy with a typical southern drawl. He had a long neck, blond hair in a pompadour, and a wide mouth, and he was the salt of the earth. Before I arrived Gifford held the record for being the skinniest man in the B-29 base. The other boys called him "The 97-Pound Wonder." But they laughed at me instead of him when we went to take an outdoor shower.

Bill Gifford was an old-timer in aviation. He was thirty-six, much older than his fellow pilots and had been flying about seventeen years. As he said, he was "too damned old to be in this bombing business." He claimed that he got so scared over Japan he could hardly think, and I imagine that was true. But I noticed he volunteered to go on a certain specially tough mission when it came up.

It turned out that Giff and I had lots of mutual friends in the early air-mail days, such as Dick Merrill and Gene Brown and Johnny Kytle, so we became practically bosom pals – The Ghandi Twins. Bill had been around in this world of aviation. He had flown the night air mail in the beginning, and then worked for Pan American in South America. He'd been in the Royal Canadian Air Force and had made seven trips across the Atlantic, ferrying bombers to England.

It was worth a theater ticket to hear Giff tell about a mission after he got back. He used his hands and his feet and half the room and a great portion of his vocabulary. He got tickled and then he got mad. It seemed that everything always went wrong when Giff was on a mission and he had an experience to prove it while I was there. (I'd gone to visit in a neighboring hut for a few minutes and he couldn't find me, or I would have been with him on it. Thank goodness I always seem to step out at the right moment.)

Anyway, it was just a half hour before supper when Giff got an emergency order to beat it to the airstrip right quick and take a ship up on a half hour's test hop. He made the flight all right, but when he got ready to land the wheels wouldn't come down. Giff radioed the held, and then began working on those wheels. Of course those big B-29s are so complicatedly automatic that you do everything by little electrical switches and levers, and not by hand. "Some guy must have spent all day crossing up wires on that airplane," Giff said when he got back. "Instead of the wheels coming down, the bomb-bay doors opened. When I tried to shut them, the upper turret gun started shooting. I hit the light switch by mistake, and the tail skid came down. Just for the hell of it I tried to lower the flaps, and instead the bomb-bay doors went shut. By that time I'd turned it over to the copilot and was back in the bomb bay trying to make some sense out of the switch-box and get things to working again. But I couldn't make head or tail out of it. I worked on the damn thing for half an hour and was gettin' madder every minute. Finally I just got so disgusted I hauled off and gave the goddam switchbox a good smack with the screw driver, and started to walk out. And just like that the wheels came down and everything was all right."

Giff looked more like a Texas cowboy than a bomber pilot. He was a conscientious objector to all forms of exercise. All the pilots slept all night and half the day, but Giff slept more than any of them. He went around most of the time in nothing but white underdrawers. He was probably the most unmilitary man in the outfit – just an old-shoe Southerner, and generous as could be. On his wall was a map of the Pacific and a picture of his wife.

The first two fingers of Gift's right hand were off, clear up to the palm. No, he didn't lose them from flak or Jap fighters. He shot them off with a shotgun when he was hunting quail many years ago. He wrote a beautiful hand by holding the pen between thumb and last two fingers. He held a beer can the same way.

Giff called his plane "Honshu Hank." He wanted to form a new fraternity called "Fujiyama, '44." Its membership would be limited to those who had flown over Japan on bombing missions in 1944. He said if he never went on another mission in his life it would suit him fine.

In my long career with the United States Army, I've made a hobby of cultivating the very best people in it. And for some strange reason the very best people usually turn out to work in the kitchen. Isn't that odd?

There in the Marianas were a Mutt and Jeff team known as Mickey and Bill who served the food in our mess hall. They had to work like dogs and they dashed around in such intent haste that you thought they were mad at everybody all the time. But they weren't; that was just a look of concentration on their faces. Whenever we gave them time to relax, they were the best-natured pair you ever saw.

The two boys were Sergeant Thomas Bill, of 3347 Belt Avenue, St. Louis, and Corporal Mickey Rovinsky, of 49 Short Street, Edwardsville, Pennsylvania. They were as different as day and night, but they worked together like cogs in a gearwheel. Sergeant Bill was tall and thin and white-skinned and had curly black hair and a sensitive face, and he didn't say much. Mickey was so short he could stand under Bill's arm, and his skin was dark. His eyes were almost shut and he talked all the time – and such talk! Mickey is unquotable, because you couldn't possibly remember things the way he said them. His colloquialisms were not sectional but pure Rovinsky. He was outspoken about his likes and dislikes and fussed back at the officers who asked for extra service, but they knew Mickey and didn't get sore about it. He was a sassy wisecracking little heart-of-gold fellow; he always wore his cap turned up in front, which gave him a cocky air. He never laughed, but he was pretty happy.

Those boys' special favorite among all the fliers was my friend Captain Bill Gifford. He was always giving them things, and sitting up and talking with them in the mess hall after supper, and as a result they'd stay up all night for him if he merely suggested it. By good fortune, I fell in with this trio and every night Giff and I would stay away from supper until the others had finished and the two boys had their tables all cleaned up and set for breakfast. Then we'd wander over through the dark and the four of us would have a banquet – such as steak and French fried potatoes. The boys would cook it and then we'd all sit down and eat, and the talk would start to fly.

The first Tokyo mission was a highlight in Mickey's life. Pilots were always tense the night before a mission, and Mickey had his troubles with them. "They took off six times for Tokyo," Mickey said. "I mean they was scheduled to go every day for six days, and they'd all be short-tempered and wanting things just so at night, and then next morning the mission would be postponed. It was their first mission up there and they'd heard a rumor there was to be 1,300 Jap fighters lined up across the sky just like a wall, and they was nervous and grumpy. Like Captain Gifford here, I can always tell when he's going the next day. He don't say much at supper like he usually does. He just wants that sharp attention and keep your mouth shut and leave him the hell alone. Well, them pilots was tense and worried and they didn't drink any beer or anything for five nights and then finally on the fifth night they was up half the night yellin' around, and then next morning they really did take off. Boy, they didn't feel good either. It's a good thing they finally went or I was gonna mutiny. I got sick and tired of puttin' grub in them damned airplanes. I was gonna refuse the seventh time. I said I'd take a court-martial before I'd put grub in them planes a seventh time. But they went that time."

Then Captain Gifford took up. "You should have been here that morning. The mission was called so fast there wasn't time to warm up the engines a few at a time, so they ran them all up at once all over the field. This whole island shook from the vibration. When I took off I had to weave around through bulldozers and between jeeps and across cane patches and I kept thinking about those 1,300 fighters we'd heard about. I sure was put out about ever getting into this business in the first place. But it turned out all right."

"When Captain Gifford gets back," Mickey went on, "he's a changed man. He's still full of nerves but he wants to talk and he wants me to keep the beer comin' out of the icebox."

Sergeant Bill sat and listened and smiled and enjoyed it and said almost nothing. He and Mickey were both married men, although they were only twenty-four and twenty-three, respectively. Bill was a truck driver and Mickey a machinist before the war. Sergeant Bill had one baby and Mickey had two. Mickey placed the birth date of his latest child by remembering it was born the night the Nips came and bombed the B-29 base the first time.

The boys had to get up at 5 a.m. and their work wasn't finished till about 9 at night. They didn't even get to go to the movies, because they never got through work in time. But they didn't seem to care. They felt they were pretty lucky to have things as nice as they were.

The day I was to leave they gave me what Mickey called my "farewell breakfast" – three fried eggs! There's nothing in this army like knowing the very best people.

Combat fliers everywhere had lots of spare time because they were under such a terrific nervous strain when they worked that they needed much recuperative rest. In the Pacific there was a triple incentive for spending practically all spare time, both waking and sleeping, in "the sack."

First, a fourteen-hour mission is an exhausting thing. The boys said the reaction was a delayed one, and they really didn't feel it keenly until the afternoon of the day after. Then they were just plumb worn out, and it took some of them two or three days to get to feeling normal.

Second, the climate, warm and enervating, made them sleepy all the time. I myself found it doubly hard to write my columns because I just couldn't stay awake.

Third, there was really nothing else to do except lie on your cot. Combat crews had few duties between missions and since there was no amusement or diversion, except homemade ones, they'd just lie and talk and lie some more. The result was that you got lazier than sin. As one pilot said, "I've got so lazy I'll never be worth a damn the rest of my life."

Troop commanders knew the importance of keeping their men busy to overcome "island neurosis," or going "pineapple crazy," but it was difficult to do that with combat crewmen. Later new classes were organized, and the fliers went to school part of each day. Those who were especially good got further intensive training as "lead crews" and went to school from morning till night.

Endless talk went on in every tent and Quonset hut. They could argue about the damnedest things. One afternoon several pilots got into a discussion over whether or not you do everything in reverse when you're flying upside down. They were all veteran fliers, and yet they split about 50-50 on whether you do or not. Another day they got to arguing about what causes planes to leave vapor trails at high altitudes. I had always thought it was the heat from the exhaust stacks condensing the moisture that whirls off the tips of the propellers. That started a long controversy in which nobody won.

They argued about God, and they recounted funny stories of escapades during training, and they wondered why the Japs didn't do this or that. Some played solitaire;, some wrote letters all the time. One flier told me he had written to people he hadn't thought of in years, not because he wanted letters back, but just to have something to do. Others, with nothing but time on their hands, couldn't make themselves write at all. They read magazines, but very few books. At first they spent weeks making furniture for themselves out of packing crates.

Some of them swam every day, and they all took daily showers. The camps were dotted with concrete-floored baths, which were roofless. Water came from tanks set on high stilts nearby. It was not heated, and although the weather is always warm, a cold bath in the morning was pretty nippy. The best time for it was around two in the afternoon when the sun had made the water good and warm.

The fliers sent some of their clothing to the Army laundry unit, but it took about ten days, so most of them did their own washing. Every bath unit had in it a white-porcelain Thor washing machine and wringer. The fliers would build a bonfire of discarded lumber, heat water in big cans, pour it into the washing machine, and turn her on. Between every two Quonset huts there was always a clothesline full of wash flying in the wind.

Some days the men played volleyball, some days they took setting-up exercises, and some days they swam. My friend Captain Bill Gifford spurned all these things, and just lay in bed. Every day they asked if he wasn't going to "P.T.," which meant physical training, and he said "Hell, no. I'm too old to get out there and jump up and down like a goddam Russian ballet dancer."

I was amazed at the number of men flying Tokyo missions in the B-29s who had already served one tour of combat duty in the European theater. Of the ten men in our hut, two were combat veterans, even though they were very young.

Major William Clark, of Bayhead, New Jersey, flew his fifty missions out of Africa in B-17s, and so did Captain Walter Kelly, of Manayunk, Pennsylvania. In fact Captain Kelly and I were together at Biskra Airdrome on the edge of the Sahara Desert two years before. They were both hardheaded, wise pilots who had learned the tropical way of wearing shorts and spending half their time lying on their cots. And they didn't seem to mind at all that they were starting all over again on this side of the world after having done their share on the other side.

One of the things most needed for morale among fliers over here was the setting up of some kind of goal for them – a definite number of combat missions to be flown and then going back to a rest camp. The way it was then, they were just flying in the dark, going on and on until Fate overtook them. The war on both sides of the world was too desperate to allow the setting up of a final mission total which would let a B-29 flier go home for good. They just went to rest camps and then came back for more missions. And the boys would just as soon lie on their own cots as to go to a rest camp. What they wanted was a change, something far away – lights and girls and companionship and modern things and gaiety.

CHAPTER FOUR

Life on a Flat-Top

I HAD my experience as a salt-water doughboy on a carrier which was part of that first strike on the Tokyo area, and which helped out at Iwo Jima too. Starting right at the beginning, I'll try to describe what living on an aircraft carrier is like, and how a big task force works when it goes out after the enemy.

First we boarded a plane and flew for a long time, landing on a tiny coral island that glared white in the tropic sun. Tall slanting palm trees waved their topknots of green fronds. The island was framed in a wide circle of bright green water and that in turn was bordered by a thin line of snow-white surf, where rolling waves beat themselves to a froth over a submerged reef. And on beyond that, everywhere as far as the eye could sec, was the heavy dark blue of the deep, deep ocean. Out there on that dark-blue water lay the United States fleet – hundreds and hundreds of ships. The Navy says officially that it was the greatest concentration of fighting ships ever assembled in the history of the world.

It was something to take your breath away. True, I have seen bigger fleets; in our invasions of both Sicily and Normandy we had more ships; but they were not predominantly warships. They were mainly landing craft and troop-carrying vessels. These, on the other hand,

43

were fighting ships – the world's mightiest. Battleships and cruisers and carriers and uncountable destroyers, and the swarm of escorts and tugs and oilers and repair ships that go with them. And this wasn't the only fleet. Others started from other anchorages scattered out over the Pacific, hundreds and thousands of miles from us. They left on a timetable schedule, so that they would all converge in the upper Pacific at the same time.

If you had felt lonely and afraid in anticipation of the ordeal upon which you were setting out, it disappeared when you became a part in this mighty armada. For when we bore down upon the waters of Japan and Iwo Jima, we were nearly a thousand ships and more than half a million men! Whatever happened to you, you would sure have a hell of a lot of company.

A small fast motorboat, its forepart covered with canvas like a prairie schooner, took me from the island to the carrier to which I had been assigned. It was a long way out, and we were half an hour bobbing up and down through the spray. Ships were so thick we had to weave in and out around them. The water was speckled with small boats running from ship to ship, and back and forth to the island. The weather was hot, and sometimes I stood up and took the spray, because it felt good.

No ship in wartime has its name painted on it. Instead, they go by numbers. Every ship in the Navy has both a name and a number, but its name is hidden for the duration. All carriers look alike to the neophyte, so you pick them out by the number on the bow. I had asked to be put on a small carrier rather than a big one. The reasons were many. For one thing, the large ones are so immense and carry such a huge crew that it would be like Grand Central Station to live in. I felt that a smaller one would give me the feel of carrier life more quickly, that I could become more intimately a member of the family. Also, the smaller carriers had had very little credit and almost no glory, and I've always had a sort of yen for poor little ships that have been neglected. And also again (although this, of course, had nothing to do with my choice, of course, of course) there was an old wives' superstition to the effect that the Japs always went for the big carriers first rather than the little ones. Further investigation revealed this to be pure fiction, but what you don't know at the time doesn't hurt you. So gaily I climbed aboard my new home – curious, but admittedly uneager for my first taste of naval warfare in the Pacific.

An aircraft carrier is a noble thing. It lacks almost everything that seems to denote nobility, yet deep nobility is there. A carrier has no poise. It has no grace. It is top-heavy and lopsided. It has the lines of a well-fed cow. It doesn't cut through the water like a cruiser, knifing romantically along. It doesn't dance and cavort like a destroyer. It just plows. You feel it should be carrying a hod. Yet a carrier is a ferocious thing, and out of its heritage of action has grown its nobility. I believe that every Navy in the world has as its No. 1 priority the destruction of enemy carriers. That's a precarious honor, but it's a proud one.

My carrier was a proud one. She was small, and you never heard of her unless you had a son or a husband on her, but still she was proud, and deservedly so. She had been at sea since November of 1943, without returning home – longer than any other carrier in the Pacific, with one exception. She was a little thing, yet her planes had shot 228 of the enemy out of the sky in air battles, and her guns had knocked down five Jap planes in defending herself. She was too proud to keep track of little ships she destroyed, but she had sent to the bottom 29 big Japanese ships. Her bombs and aerial torpedoes had smashed into everything from the greatest Jap battleships to the tiniest coastal schooners.

She had weathered five typhoons. Her men had not set foot on any soil bigger than a farm-sized uninhabited atoll for a solid year. They had not seen a woman, white or otherwise, for nearly ten months. In a year and a quarter out of America, she had steamed a total of 149,000 miles! Four different air squadrons had used her as their flying field, flown their allotted missions, and returned to America. But the ship's crew stayed on – and on, and on.

She was known in the fleet as "The Iron Woman," because she had fought in every battle in the Pacific in 1944 and every one to date in 1945. Her battle record sounded like the map of the Pacific war – Kwajalein, Eniwetok, Truk, Palau, Hollandia, Saipan, Chichi Jima, Mindanao, Luzon, Formosa, Nansei Shoto, Hong Kong, Iwo Jima, Tokyo, and many others.

She had known disaster. Her fliers who had perished could not be counted on both hands, yet the ratio was about as it always was – approximately one American lost for every ten of the Exalted Race sent to the Exalted Heaven. She had been hit twice by Jap bombs. She had had mass burials at sea … with her dry-eyed crew sewing to the corpses of their friends 40-millimeter shells as weights to take them to the bottom of the sea. Yet she had never even returned to Pearl Harbor to mend her wounds. She slapped on some patches on the run, and was ready for the next battle. The crew in semi-jocularity cussed her chief engineer for keeping her in such good shape that they had no excuse to go back to Honolulu or America for overhaul.

My carrier, even though classed as "light," was still a very large ship. She was more than 700 feet long and over 1,000 men dwelt upon her. She had all the facilities of a small city, and all the gossip and small talk too. Latest news and rumors reached the farthest cranny of the ship a few minutes after the captain himself knew about them. All she lacked was a hitching rack and a town pump with a handle.

She had five barbers, a laundry, a general store. Deep in her belly she carried tons of bombs. She had a daily newspaper. She carried fire-fighting equipment that a city of 50,000 back in America would be proud of. She had a preacher, she had three doctors and two dentists, she had two libraries, and movies every night except when in battle. And still she was a tiny thing, as the carriers go. She was a "baby flat-top."

She had been out so long that her men put their ship above their captain. They saw captains come and go, but they and the ship stayed on forever. They weren't romantic about their long stay. They hated it, and their gripes were long and loud. They yearned pathetically to go home. But down underneath they were proud – proud of their ship and proud of themselves.

The second day I was aboard, the chief steward came up to my cabin and announced happily that he had a cake for me, but it was so big he didn't know how to handle it. For a while I couldn't get what he was driving at, but finally he made it clear. It seemed the night bakers had made a huge cake for me, to be served at dinner that evening. The steward was worried because the cake was so big they didn't have a board big enough to put it on, and therefore they couldn't put it on the table where everybody could see it. But that evening when we went down to dinner, there was the cake in front of my chair, right in the middle of the table and almost filling it up. They had solved the problem by getting the carpenters to make a board. Written in pink icing on top of the white cake were the words: "Welcome aboard, Mr. Pyle." I was so taken aback at being called "Mr. Pyle" that I didn't recognize the name at first.

I was pleased and embarrassed by this first official cake of my lifetime, and of course I had to take a lot of ribbing from my friends. They said they'd been slaving on that damn ship for a year and nobody had ever baked a special cake for them. One of the ship's photographers came and took pictures of me ostensibly cutting the cake when I wasn't cutting it at all. And then we ate it.

After supper I groped my way through the labyrinth of passages below, and finally tracked down the thoughtful person who had baked the cake. He was Ray Conner, Baker Second Class from LeGrande, Oregon. LeGrande is in eastern Oregon not far from Pendleton, and Ray was mourning that he hadn't seen the famous Pendleton Roundup for three years. I asked him how he happened to bake a cake for me, and he said, well, he had got through his regular baking a little early the night before and hadn't anything else to do, and just thought it was a good idea. Ray's father was a schoolteacher, and Ray had studied to be one, but he rather doubted he would want to teach school after the war.

If I had to be in the Navy, I think I'd about as soon be a baker as anything else. The bakeshop is always dean as a whistle, and it always smells good. And you are practically your own boss. Ray was quite satisfied with his lot in the Navy, mainly because a bakery is so wonderfully clean. "I can't stand to work in filth," he said.

I was feeling pretty stuck-up about my cake, and then next evening when we went down to supper there was a big cake on the adjoining table. I made a few discreet inquiries as to who had the gall to have a cake in front of him so soon after my triumph. And I learned it was for the pilot who, the day before, had made the 8,000th landing on our carrier. It seemed a cake was a tradition for every thousandth landing.

After the meal I went around and introduced myself to this cad. He was Lieutenant VanVranken, of Stockton, California. I said, "I'm plenty sore. I thought I was the only one around here who rated a cake."

And he said, "Well, I'm jealous. You had photographers taking pictures of your cake. But could I get a photographer? No."

So I said, "Well, that's better. So you made the 8,000th landing? Was it a good one?"

He grinned and said, "Well, I got aboard." And then he added, "As a matter of fact, it was a pretty good landing. And if you're ever in California after the war, come to Stockton and we'll have something better than cake."

Lieutenant VanVranken was no amateur at landing on carriers. He had made around 120 carrier landings before he came on our ship, and by that time his total was up around 200. A guy who makes that many landings on a carrier and is still making them didn't learn it in correspondence school.

Eight thousand landings is small stuff for the big carriers. Some of them are lots older, and also they have three times as many planes to land every day. I think the record on our oldest carriers is something up around 80,000. But we liked 8,000 on our ship, and anyhow we didn't have enough flour for eighty cakes.

The first time you see a plane land on a carrier you almost die. At the end of the first day my muscles were sore just from being all tensed up while watching the planes come in. It is so fast, timing is so split-second, space is so small – well, somebody said that carrier pilots were the best in the world, and they must be or there wouldn't be any of them left alive.

Planes don't approach a carrier as they would land – from way back and in a long glide. Instead, they almost seem to be sneaking up as if to surprise it. They're in such an awkward position and Hying at such a crazy angle you don't see how they can ever land on anything. But it's been worked out by years of experience, and it's the best way.

Everything is straightened out in the last few seconds of flying. That is – if it works.

Anything can happen in those first few seconds. Once in a great while the plane loses its speed and spins into the water just behind the ship. And planes have been known to ram right into the stern. The air currents are always bad. The ship's "island" distorts the currents, and makes the air rough. Even the wake of the ship – the water churned up by the propellers – has an effect on the air through which the planes must pass.

If half a dozen planes come in successively without one getting a "wave off" from the signalman, you're doing pretty well. For landing on the deck of a small carrier in a rough sea is just about like landing on half a block of Main Street while a combination hurricane and earthquake is going on.

You call it a perfect landing if a plane comes in and hits on both wheels at the same time, in the center of the deck headed straight forward and catching about the third one of the cables stretched across the deck. But very few of them are perfect. They come in a thousand different ways, and if their approach is too bad, the signalman waves them around again.

They'll sometimes come in too fast and hit the deck so hard a tire blows. They'll come in half-sideways, and the cable will jerk them around in a tire-screeching circle. They'll, come in too close to the edge of the deck, and sometimes go right on over into the catwalk. They'll come in so high they'll miss all the arresting gear and slam into the high cables stretched across mid-decks, called "the barrier." Sometimes they do a somersault over the barrier, and land on their backs. Sometimes they bounce all around and hit the island. Sometimes they bounce fifty feet in the air and still get down all right. Sometimes they catch fire.

During the Tokyo strike, one of the big carriers running near us lost three planes in ten minutes. One was shot up and had to ditch in the water alongside the ship. The next one slammed into the island, and was so wrecked they just heaved the wreckage over the side. The next one to come in crashed the barrier and burned up.

49

On the other hand, you'll land planes for weeks without a bad crackup. We wrecked three planes in crashes our first three days out – and not a single one after that.

The first time I watched our boys land they were pretty bad. They hadn't flown for about two weeks and were a little rusty. It's always that way after a ship has been in port for a while. Everybody dreads the first two or three days.

As I was watching the first flight coming in one by one, my roommate, Lieutenant Commander Al Masters, came up behind me and said, "Well, I see you've got the carrier stance already. I noticed you leaning way over to help pull them around into position."

When all the planes were back, I walked over to Commander Al Gurney, the air officer, and said, "If I'm going to watch this for the whole trip, you'll have to provide me with some heart-failure medicine."

And he replied, "Well, think of me. I've had to watch two thousand of them. It'll drive you nuts."

The previous skipper of our ship finally got so he refused to watch when the planes were coming in. He just stood on the bridge and kept looking forward. And a friend of mine in the crew was almost as bad. He was Chief Bosun's Mate George Rowe, from 3301 Chenault Street, Fort Worth, Texas. His nickname was "Catfish."

"I was on this ship for a year before I ever saw an entire flight land," he said. "I just couldn't bear to look at them." But as the trip wore on, the boys improved and my own nerves hardened, and between us we managed to get all our planes down for the rest of the trip without a single casualty either to them or to me.

There was nothing dramatic about our start for Japan. We simply pulled anchor about eight o'clock one morning and got underway. The whole thing seemed peaceful and routine. Our ships were so spread out that they didn't seem as overpowering as they actually were. It wasn't like the swarming, pulsing mass that literally blanketed the water when we started to Sicily and to Normandy. Once at sea our force broke up into several prearranged units and each put some distance between itself and the next. Each was self-sufficient, complete unto itself. Each had battleships, carriers, cruisers, and destroyers. Each could protect itself.

The eye could easily encompass the formation in which we were sailing. And very dimly, far off on the horizon, we could see the silhouettes of the bigger ships on each side of us, although they seemed remote and not like neighbors. The rest of the fleet was out of sight, far over the horizon. Altogether, the ships must have covered a hundred miles of ocean. The formations were commanded by admirals and above them all was Admiral Marc Mitscher.

All day and all night the air was full of conversation among our ships. Messages were transmitted in many ways – by signal flag, by light blinker, by destroyers bringing written messages, and even by planes flying slowly over and dropping messages on the deck.

The admiral commanding our unit was a fine, friendly man whom I'd met before we sailed. On the third day out he sent a message over to our captain which said: "How is Ernie getting along? Does he wish he was back in a foxhole?" We messaged back that I was happy, hadn't been seasick yet, and that I hoped all my future foxholes could be as plush as this one.

We kept radio silence – that is, we didn't send any long-distance radio messages – to keep the Japs from learning where we were. We had a long way to go from our I starting point, and our route was a devious one to boot, and we steamed for several days before we were at our destination off Japan. We sailed long enough to have crossed the Atlantic Ocean – if we had been in the Atlantic.

But those days were busy ones. Our planes began operating as soon as we were underway. Three fighters that had been based on the island Hew out and landed aboard an hour after we started, to fill our complement of planes. We were up before dawn every morning, and our planes were in the air before sunup. We kept a constant aerial patrol over our ships. Some flew at great height, completely out of sight. Others took the medium altitude. And still others roamed in great circles only a few hundred feet above us. Out on the perimeter our little destroyers plowed the ocean, always alert for subs or planes. You really couldn't help but feel safe with such a guard around you.

Living was very comfortable aboard ship. I shared a cabin with Lieutenant Commander Al Masters from Terre Haute, Indiana, which is just a few miles from where I was born and raised. In cur cabin we had metal closets and writing desks and a lavatory with hot and cold water. We had a telephone, and a colored boy to clean up the room. Our bunks were double-decked, with good mattresses; I was in the upper one. The food was wonderful, and we could buy a whole carton of cigarettes a day if we wanted to. We saw a movie every night except when in battle. The first four nights our movies were *New York Town*, *The Major and the Minor*, *Spring Fever*, and *Claudia*. I didn't know enough about movies to know whether they were old or not, but it doesn't make any difference to a sailor who hasn't been home.

I came aboard with a lot of dirty clothes, for I'd had nothing washed since leaving San Francisco about a month before. Our cabin boy took my clothes to the laundry about 9:30 one morning. When I came back to the cabin an hour and a half later, there was my washing all clean and dry and ironed, lying on the bed. What a ship!

It's easy to get acquainted aboard a naval vessel. The sailors were just as friendly as the soldiers I'd known on the other side. Furthermore, they were so delighted to see a stranger and have somebody new to talk to that they weren't a bit standoffish.

They were all sick to death of the isolation and monotony of the vast Pacific. I believe they talked even more about wanting to go home than the soldiers in Europe. Their lives really were empty; they had their work, their movies, and their mail, and that's just about all they did have. And nothing to look forward to. They never saw anybody but themselves. They sailed and sailed, and never arrived anywhere; they hadn't even seen a village for a year. Three times they'd been to remote, lifeless sand bars in the Pacific, and had been allowed to go ashore for a few hours and sit under palm trees and drink three cans of beer. That's all.

Yet they did live well. Their food was the best I had had in this war. They had steaks and ice cream – they probably ate better than they would at home. They had daily baths, and the laundry washed their clothes. The quarters were crowded, but each man had a bunk with mattress and sheets, and a private locker to keep his stuff in. They worked hard, but their hours were regular.

The boys asked a thousand times how it compared with the other side. I could only answer that it was much better. They seemed to expect me to say that, but they were a little disappointed too. They said, "But it's tough to be away from home for more than a year, and never see anything but water and an occasional atoll." And I said, yes, I knew it was, but there were boys who had been in Europe more than three years, and had slept on the ground a good part of that time. And they said, yes, they guessed their lives were pretty good by contrast.

Seaman Paul Begley looked at his wartime life philosophically. He was a farm boy from Rogersville, Tennessee, and his job was that of plane pusher on the flight deck. He talked a lot in a soft voice that was clear southern. "I can stand this monotony all right," he said. "The point with us is that we've got a pretty good chance of living through this. Think of the Marines who have to take the beaches, and the infantry in Germany. I can stand a lot of monotony if I know my chances are pretty good for coming out of it alive." But others yelled their heads off, and felt they were being persecuted by being kept out of America a year. I heard some boys say, "I'd trade this for a foxhole any day." You just have to keep your mouth shut to a remark like that.

At least fifty per cent of the sailors' conversation, when talking to a newcomer like myself, was about three tilings: the terrible typhoon they went through off the Philippines; the times they were hit by Jap bombs; and their desire to get back to America.

The typhoon was awful. Many thought they would go the same way as the three destroyers that capsized; the ship was inclined to roll badly anyhow. She still had immense dents in her smokestacks where they smacked the water when she rolled that far over. A lot of experienced sailors were seasick during that storm.

Very few of the boys had developed any real love for the sea – the kind that would draw them back to it for a lifetime. Some of course will come back if things get tough' after the war. But mostly they were temporary sailors, and the sea was not in their blood. Taking it all in all, they were good boys who did what was asked of them, and did it well. And they were almost unanimously proud of their ship.

I think I was asked a hundred times how I happened to come on their ship, with so many to choose from. It was always said in that tone that meant they hoped I chose it because it had such a noble reputation. So I told them that I asked to be put on a light carrier, rather than a big one, and that, being a newcomer to the Pacific, I didn't know one ship from another, and theirs was the ship the Navy put me on. But that satisfied them just as well, for then they assumed that the Navy itself considered their ship a superior one – which I'm sure it did.

The men aboard an aircraft carrier can be divided into three groups. There are the fliers, both officer-pilots and enlisted radiomen and gunners, who actually fly in combat. They do nothing but fly, and study, and prepare to fly. Then there are the men who maintain the fliers. The air officers, and the mechanics, and the many plane handlers who shift and push the planes a dozen times a day around the deck. These men are ordinarily known as "Airedales," but the term wasn't much used on our ship; usually they just called themselves "plane pushers." And third is the ship's crew – the deck hands, engineers, signalmen, cooks, plumbers, and barbers. They run the ship, just as though it were any ship in the Navy.

The fliers aren't looked upon as gods by the rest of the crew, but they are respected. Hardly a man on the crew would trade places with them. They've seen enough crash landings on deck to know what the fliers go through.

But there is a feeling – a slight one – between the ship's regular crew and the air maintenance crew. The ship's crew consider that the plane handlers think they're prima donnas. One said to me, "Them Airedales is the ones that gets all the glory. Nobody ever hears about us. All we do is keep the damn ship going." But as far as I could see, the Airedales haven't had an awful lot of glory. And their job is often a miserable one. Their hours are ungodly, and in the pinches they work like fiends. I think the Airedale deserves what little credit he gets.

It is these plane pushers who make the flight deck of an aircraft carrier look as gay and wildly colorful as a Walt Disney cartoon, for they dress in bright colors. They wear cloth helmets and sweaters that are blue, green, red, yellow, white or brown. This colorful gear isn't just a whim. Each color identifies a special type of workman, so that they can be picked out quickly and sent on hurried tasks.

Red is the gasoline and fire-fighting detail. Blue is for the guys who just push the planes around. Brown is for plane captains and mechanics. White stands for radiomen and the engineering bosses. Yellow is for the plane directors. Yellow is what a pilot looks for the moment he gets on deck. For the plane directors guide him as though they were leading a blind man. They use a sign language with their hands that is the same all over the Navy, and by obeying their signs explicitly the pilot can taxi his plane within two inches of another one without ever looking at it.

All the pilots and ship's officers live in "officers' country" in the forward part of the ship – comfortable cabins, housing from one to four men. The crew lives in compartments of all shapes and sizes. Some hold as little as half a dozen men; others are big and house a hundred men. The Navy doesn't use hammocks any more. Every man has a bed and it is called a "rack." It's merely a tubular framework, with wire springs stretched across it. Attached to the wall by hinges, it is folded up against the wall in the daytime. The racks aren't let down till about seven in the evening (except for men standing regular watch who must sleep in the daytime) ; hence a sailor has no regular place to sit or lie down during the day if he does nab a few spare minutes.

A light carrier, such as ours, had only about a third as many planes as the big carriers, and less than half the crew, but it did exactly the same kind of work. Of the three types of carriers in the Navy, ours had the narrowest flight deck of all. It was so narrow that when planes took off they used the left side of the deck so that their right wingtip wouldn't come too close to the island as they passed.

Our pilots and crew were quite proud that we had the narrowest flight deck in existence. They were proud they could even hit the damn thing. They enjoyed telling this story, for example: One day one of our planes had engine trouble and couldn't make it back to our ship. It had to land on the carrier nearest to it, which happened to be a big one. The pilot circled around it and radioed in, asking permission to land. When the permission came back, he sent another message, facetiously inquiring: "Which runway?"

• • •

We were launching our midmorning patrol flight. The sun was out bright, and the day magnificently warm. Everything was serene. I had already become acquainted with some of the pilots, and before each flight I would go to the "ready room" and find out from the blackboard the numbers of the planes they were flying, so I could identify them as they went past.

Lieutenant Jimmy Van Fleet was one of the pilots I knew best. We got acquainted because we had a mutual friend – War Correspondent Chris Cunningham, with whom I shared a tent and sometimes worse through Tunisia and Sicily and Italy. Jimmy and Chris were from the same town – Findlay, Ohio.

We knew the very moment he started that Jimmy was in trouble. His plane veered sharply to the right, and a big puff of white smoke spurted from his right brake band. Then slowly the plane turned and angled to the left as it gained speed. The air officer up in the island sensed catastrophe, and put his hand on the warning squawker. All the sailors standing on the catwalk, with their heads sticking up over the edge of the flight deck, quickly ducked down. Yet such is the rigidity of excitement that I never even heard the squawker.

It was obvious Jimmy couldn't stop his plane from going to the left. His right wheel was locked, and the tire was leaving burned rubber on the deck, yet it wouldn't turn the plane. And it was too late for him to stop now. It had to happen. About midway of the flight deck, exactly opposite from where I was standing, he went over the side at full tilt, with his engine roaring. His wheels raked the antiaircraft guns, his propeller missed men's heads by inches, his left wing dropped, and in a flash he had disappeared. It all happened in probably no more than six seconds. I had stood frozen while it went on, eyes glued to the inevitable. We all thought it was the end for Jimmy.

When the plane again came into view, only the tail was sticking out of the water. And then Jimmy bobbed up beside it. He had got out in a few seconds. "Get your smoke bombs over," the air officer boomed to the crew over the loud-speaker. Those were to mark his position for any ship that would pick him up.

When he got back, Jimmy told me what happened from there on. He said that when the plane went into the water it went so deep that it got dark in the cockpit. Jimmy wasn't hurt by the crash, outside of a small cut on his forehead. He pulled his various buckles, opening his hatch cover and releasing himself from his seat harness. But as he did so he fell forward (the plane was riding nose down in the water, of course) and in a moment he was standing on his head, underwater, and in a hell of a fix. Somehow he got himself upright, but then he couldn't get out because his radio cord, attached to his helmet, was still plugged into its socket back of his seat. So he took his big sheath knife out of its holder, cut the radio cord and carefully put the knife back. He says he doesn't know why he put it back. AH this happened underwater, and in mere seconds. Some part of his clothing caught as he was getting out, and he gave a big yank to free himself, tearing his Mae West wide open, both compartments of it, so that he had no buoyancy at all. But he is an excellent swimmer, so he managed to stay up.

When Jimmy went over the side, a destroyer was running about a mile to our left. Here again Jimmy was lucky, for that wasn't the destroyer's normal position; it just happened to be cutting across the convoy to deliver some mail on the other side. Jimmy had hardly hit the water when we saw the destroyer heel over in a swath-cutting turn. They had been watching the takeoffs through their glasses, and had seen him go over. Our own ship, of course, had to keep going straight ahead. And our next plane took off without the slightest wait, as though nothing had happened.

The destroyer had Jimmy aboard in just seven minutes. They didn't put over a boat for him, but instead sent a swimmer out with a line tied around his waist. He got there just in time; Jimmy passed out in his arms. With no lifebelt, he had taken too much salt water aboard. In the meantime the destroyer had let down a metal stretcher, and another swimmer was there to help get Jimmy into it. It took a while for them to get him on, for he was dead weight, and the stretcher kept going up and down with the waves. But finally they managed it. Jimmy was safe and alive, although a very water-laden and unconscious young man.

Destroyers love to pick up airplane pilots out of the ocean. When they rescued Jimmy it was pilot rescue No. 15 for them. Destroyers keep a box score on it, just as carriers keep score of the planes they shoot down. They even keep records of their speed, and try to set a new record. Their record rescue was three minutes.

They put Jimmy to bed, got the water out of him and some morphine into him, and sewed up the gash in his head. The doctor joked as he sewed, telling Jimmy he was sorry he couldn't find a bigger needle so it would hurt more. Jimmy was nightmarish all night. He didn't get sick at his stomach until next morning, when he tried to get some breakfast down, he had a headache next day, but after that he was all right.

Destroyers treat rescued pilots as though they were kings. They put Jimmy up in the skipper's private cabin, since the skipper was on the bridge day and night anyhow. Jimmy wore the skipper's bathrobe and house slippers and underwear. The skipper came in a couple of times to take a bath, and actually apologized for intruding. Fishing out pilots was such a frequent occurrence that the skipper even kept a bundle of brand-new toothbrushes in his medicine cabinet for such sudden guests.

By the time Jimmy came to, the laundry had washed and pressed his clothes. He didn't have his wallet, so his pictures and private papers were spared a dunking.

This particular destroyer had fished out so many pilots that they had a scroll already printed up, and all they had to do was fill in the name. It was a picturesque certificate something like what you get when you cross the equator. Across the top of Jimmy's scroll were engraved the words: "The Blank's Home for Dripping Aviators." And beneath it was this: "Know ye that Lieutenant James Van Fleet on such and such a date abruptly appeared in our happy home, and due to the peculiarities of his arrival has been found worthy of being honored as a Blank's dripping aviator." Engraved over the scroll was a huge arm reaching out from a destroyer, hauling a wet flier out of the ocean by the seat of his pants.

They returned Jimmy to us three days later, when they were delivering messages and mail from the flagship. They sent him over in a bosun's chair, pulled across on a heavy line strung between the two ships. We got Jimmy aboard, and then we sent twenty gallons of ice cream back across in the chair to the destroyer. Our carrier always did that when a destroyer rescued one of her pilots. Apparently all carriers don't, for the destroyer sent back a scribbled note: "Thanks a lot. That is the nicest thing that has ever happened to us."

After we heard the whole story, we sent a signal back to the destroyer asking for the names of the two men who rescued our pilot. The destroyer came right back: The swimmer was Seaman First Class Franklin Calloway, of 4633 Oakland Street, Philadelphia, and the one who helped was Radioman Third Class Melvin Collins, of 102 North Vine Street, Ottumwa, Iowa.

They were smart on that destroyer. A few hours later there came another message: "If that information is for the press, might add that both men received Bronze Stars for similar rescue work during operations off Leyte last fall."

Jimmy Van Fleet was twenty-five, and had been a schoolteacher before he became a fighter pilot in the Navy. His home in Findlay was at 327 College Street, but his wife was living at 339 North Main Street, Kenton, Ohio. He had a son seven months old whom he had never seen. Jimmy asked me if I had ever been in Vienna. His father was a Pfc. in the last war, had spent three years in a hospital in Vienna, and had always wanted to go back. It was his dream city.

Jimmy's only brother, Ensign Donald Van Fleet, also a carrier pilot, had been killed off Formosa just a few months before. He had got two Jap planes in the two weeks before he himself was shot down. We were grateful that the sea gave Jimmy back.

One of the first friends I made aboard ship was a tall, well-built, mustached sailor named Jerry Ryan. He wore dungarees, smoked a pipe sometimes, and always wore his sleeves rolled up. He was from 716 West Locust Street, Davenport, Iowa, but his wife was living in Indianapolis. He was a boilermaker first class. Jerry had served one hitch in the Navy before the war and he knew all the little ins and outs of how to get along. Everybody liked him. He wasn't especially talkative, yet it's safe to say he knew more people than anybody else on the ship.

Ryan was what is known in the Navy as "a good man": skilled in his work, dependable, and very smart. He'd die before he'd curry favor with anybody. He was the kind an officer could depend on utterly – if that officer played square with Ryan. But he caught on to a phoney so quickly it would make your head swim.

Ryan's concept of right and wrong was very precise, and the Irish in him didn't hesitate when a crisis came. The other boys told me of an incident that occurred on one of the days when Jap bombs hit the ship, off the Philippines. A great hole was torn in the deck. Several men were killed, and many wounded. Bodies of their comrades were still lying mangled on the deck when a sailor came up to look at the damage, and said almost exultingly, "Oh, boy, this is great. Now at last they'll have to send us back to America for repairs."

Without saying a word, Ryan turned and knocked him down.

Ryan ran what is known as the "oil shack." From this little domain the condensers were regulated. He had dials and gauges and a phone and a clipboard on which were kept hourly records of oil pressures and water levels and all such. The shack was a little room about the size of an apartment kitchenette, with a metal workbench and drawers full of tools, and one folding canvas stool.

Ryan's oil shack was a social center; somebody was always hanging around. You could get a cup of coffee there, look at seashell collections, see card tricks, or find out the latest rumors that had started on the bridge five minutes ago. Jerry brewed coffee for his guests over an electric grill in a nickel-plated pot which had a red hash mark for one hitch of service in the Navy. It had got dented in the Philippines typhoon. And soon he was going to award it the Purple Heart.

Some nights we popped corn in the oil shack. The boys' folks sent them corn in cans, and they begged butter from the galley, and popped 'er up in a skillet on the grill. One of Ryan's friends who came to eat popcorn was a Negro – a tall, athletic fellow from his home town of Davenport. They were on the ship together for a year before they found out they were from the same place. The colored boy's name was Wesley Cooper and he was a cook. He had been a star athlete hack home and was the best basketball player in the whole crew. He had a scholarship waiting for him at the University of Iowa.

Wesley came down to the shack almost every night after supper. He smoked a curved-stem pipe, holding one hand up to it and listening and grinning and not saying much. We were popping corn one night. One of the boys said. "Wes, how about getting us some more butter?" And another one said, "Wes, bring some salt, will you?" And a third said, "And bring me a sandwich when you come down, will you, Wes?" And Wes grinned and his white teeth flashed and he said, "I suppose you'd like for me to go up and cook you a whole meal?" He never made a move.

Another of my best friends was Howard Wilson, a bosun's mate second class. Like Lieutenant Jimmy Van Fleet, he was from Findlay, Ohio, and in fact they were good friends. Wilson was a soft-spoken, handsome, highly intelligent man of thirty-five. Back in Findlay he had a beautiful home and a good business as part owner and general manager of three movie theaters. His wife was running them while he was away. In those bygone years back in the old home town, Jimmy Van Fleet used to borrow money from Howard Wilson when he got hard up. But now the younger Jimmy dwelt in the comparative luxury of officers' quarters, and the older Howard lived the lowlier life of a sailor, sleeping on a rack in a crowded compartment and wearing dungarees.

That's the way things go in wartime. Howard was old and wise and it didn't bother him in the slightest. He accepted the war and his own lot calmly. The other pilots knew of their friendship, and asked Jimmy if he was keeping on the good side of Howard to assure himself of a job when the war was over. He said he was.

There are moments when a voyage to war has much of the calm and repose of a pleasure cruise in peacetime. Day after day we sailed in seas that were smooth and warm, under benign skies. There was no air of urgency about us. True, we kept air patrols in the sky, but it was really a practice gesture, for we were far away from the enemy. Sailors at work wore no shirts. Little bunches of flying fish skimmed the blue water. You needed dark glasses on deck. Pilots took sun baths on the forecastle. Up on the broad flight deck, clad only in shorn, the chaplain and executive officer were playing deck tennis. And in the afternoon the forward elevator was let down, and officers and men played basketball. Every night we had movies after supper. It was hard to keep it in mind that we were a ship of war, headed for war.

Then ever so gradually the weather changed, as we plowed northward. The day before and all the days behind it had been tropically hot. Today was surprisingly and comfortably cool. Tomorrow would be cold. We were nearing the Great Hunting Grounds off Japan.

On the last day you could sense the imminence of it all over the ship. Not by anything big, but by the little things. Our weeks of monotony and waiting were at an end. The daily briefings of the pilots became more detailed. There was less playboyishness among the crew. Ordinary ship's rules were changed to battle rules. What is known as the "extended action bill" went into effect. Sailors could let down their racks in the daytime, and get a little extra rest. Meal hours, instead of being at 12 and 6 o'clock sharp, were changed to run from 11 till 1, and from 4:30 to 6:30, so that men on watch could trade off and dash in for a bite. The captain never left the bridge, either to eat or to sleep.

When we went into our cabin, we found our bunks had been made up with "flash sheets" around them. They are black rubberized sheets, to protect the men from bomb burns. Everybody was issued "flash gear." That consists of several items – a thin gray hood that covers the head and hangs down over the shoulders; a white cloth on an elastic band to cover the nose and mouth; isinglass goggles; and long gray cloth gloves with a high gauntlet. All this was to save the hands and face from the searing, flame-throwing blast of a big shell or bomb when it exploded. On some ships the men painted their faces with an anti-flash grease, which made them look like circus clowns, but they didn't on our ship.

On the lower decks, every compartment door was closed, so that, it a torpedo should hit, it would flood only the compartment where it struck. All the rest of the ship would be sealed off from it. The ship's hospital was shut off, and the medics set up business in the many prearranged aid stations scattered about higher decks of the ship. They could even perform operations at any one of a dozen temporary spots in mess halls or cabins.

Also we broke out cold-weather gear for the bone-chilling days ahead. Extra blankets were put on our bunks. Blue Navy sweaters came out for the first time, and blue stocking caps, and several kinds of rain capes with parkas to pull over the head. You even saw a few pea jackets. We had long underwear too. It had never been used before, and goodness knows how long it had been baled up in shipboard stockrooms, for some of it was mildewed. In fact, the suit they got out for the captain – well, they had to wash and dry it hurriedly before giving it to him, because it smelled so badly from mildew.

After supper on the night before our strike, we saw the movie *The Magnificent Dope*. I guess it was old, but it was good and awfully funny. At least we thought so; everybody laughed hilariously. When tension builds up in a man before a period of great danger, the tension is not usually visible. That's the way it was that night, except that I noticed there were only half as many people at the movie as usual. And not long after it was over everybody had gone to bed. They knew there would be no rest the next day.

We were up an hour and a half before daylight, since our planes had to be in the air at the first hint of dawn. The first patrol was always launched by catapult, because in the wind-swept semi-darkness it was too dangerous to make the run down the rolling deck.

After seeing the flights launched the first few days, it had become old stuff. I would have stayed in bed and ignored it, but that was impossible; the catapults huge launching machinery was directly above my cabin, and every time it shot a plane off it was just as though the Washington Monument had fallen on the ship. Rip Van Winkle himself couldn't have slept through it, so I just got up.

The fighter pilots were given their last briefing. In the ready room the squadron commander and intelligence officer showed them on maps and by drawings on the blackboards just where they would strike. The squadron commander asked how many of the pilots had no wrist watches. Six held up their hands. Since the ship had no extra wrist watches, I don't know why he asked the question in the first place.

Then he told approximately what our total of planes over Japan would be, and how many the Japs might put up against us. He said, "So, you see, each one of us will only have to take care of three Jap planes!" The pilots all laughed and looked at each other sheepishly. (Days later, when the final scores were in, we found our force had destroyed Japs at nine to one.) And at the end of the briefing, the squadron commander gave strict orders for pilots not to shoot at Japs coming down in parachutes. "They're supposed to do it to us," he said, "but it isn't the thing for us to do."

The bomber pilots and their enlisted gunners and radiomen were briefed the same way. After the intelligence officer had finished, the squadron commander said, "We're going to dive low on the target before releasing our bombs. Since we're risking our necks anyhow, there's no point in going at all unless we can do some damage, so go down low."

All through the various strikes on Japan, our task force kept back enough planes to fly a constant blanket of protection in the sky above us. I remember the funny sign chalked on the blackboard of the ready room that first day, urging our patrol pilots to extra vigilance against Jap planes that might sneak out from the mainland to attack us. The sign said: "Keep alert – remember your poor scared pals on the ship!"

We didn't know whether the first of our planes over the mainland would surprise the Japs or not. It hardly seemed possible; yet there were no indications that they knew we were there. For two days during our approach we had been knocking off Jap reconnaissance planes and picket boats, and we hoped we had got these scattered planes and boats before they could radio back home the news of our presence. One of our destroyers had even sat all day on top of a Jap submarine to keep him from coming to the top and sending a warning. But still we didn't know for sure, so there was tenseness that first morning. We knew almost exactly what time our planes would first be over the Tokyo area.

We went to the radio room to listen. The usual Japanese programs were on the air. We watched the clock. Suddenly – at just the right time – the Jap stations all went off the air. There was silence for a few minutes. And then the most Donald-Ducklike screaming and jabbering you ever heard. The announcer was so excited we had to laugh.

We knew our boys were there. After that, for us on the ship, it was just a matter of waiting, and hoping. And, as the blackboard sign said, of being poor scared pals.

All but six of our planes were back from their strike on Tokyo and safely landed. The six formed a separate flight, and we couldn't believe that all of them had been lost, so our officers didn't feel too concerned. And then came a radio message from the flight leader. One of the six was down in the ocean, and the other five were hanging around to try to direct some surface vessel to his rescue. That's all we knew for hours.

When we finally got the story, this was it: Ensign Robert Buchanan, of Clementon, New Jersey, was hit by flak as they were diving on their target some twenty miles west of Tokyo. Buchanan himself was not hurt. He kept his plane up till he got over water, but it was still very much Japanese water. In fact, it was in Tokyo's outer bay – the bigger one of the two bays leading in to Tokyo. Ensign Buchanan was an ace, with five Jap planes to his credit. He ditched his plane successfully, and got out in his rubber boat. He was only eight miles from shore, and five miles from the big island that stands at the bay entrance.

Then the flight leader took charge. He was Lieutenant John Fecke, of Duxbury, Massachusetts. He was also an ace, and an old hand at the game. He had downed seven Jap planes. Fecke took the remaining four of the flight, and started out looking for an American rescue ship. They found one about thirty miles off the bay entrance. They talked to it on the radio, told the circumstances, and received word that the ship was willing to try, but wanted the fliers to stick with him and give air support. So Lieutenant Fecke ordered the other four to stay and circle above the ship while he went back to pick up Buchanan's location and guard him. But when he got there, he couldn't find Buchanan. He flew for twenty-five minutes around Tokyo Bay and was about to despair when he began getting sun flashes in his eyes. He flew about three miles more and there was Buchanan. He had used his signal mirror, just the way it says in the book.

In the meantime, the ship's progress was slow. It took almost two hours to get there, and one by one the aerial escort began getting in trouble, and one by one Fecke ordered them home to our ship, which was getting farther away all the time.

Lieutenant Irl Sonner, of Petaluma, California, lost the use of his radio, and had to leave. Lieutenant Max Barnes, of Olympia, Washington, got dangerously low on gas, and Fecke sent him home. Gas shortage also sent back Lieutenant Bob Murray of Muncie, Indiana. That left only Lieutenant Fecke circling above the man in the boat, and Lieutenant Arnold Berner, of Springdale, Arkansas, flying lone aerial escort for the rescue ship.

Finally the ship was past the bay entrance. The skipper began to have his doubts. He had to go within three miles of the gun-dotted island; he was within five minutes' flying distance of land, and Jap planes could butcher him. Furthermore, he looked at his chart, and saw that he was in "restricted waters," meaning they were probably mined. It was certainly no place for a ship to be.

The skipper radioed Fecke and said he couldn't go any farther. Fecke radioed back and said, "It's only two miles more. Please try."

The skipper answered and said, "Okay, we'll try."

And they pulled it off. They went right into the lion's mouth, pulled out our pilot, and got safely away. Then, and then only, did Fecke and Berner start home. They came back to us three hours after all the rest had returned. They had flown six hours on a three-hour mission, but they helped save an American life by doing so.

That night I lay in my bunk reading a copy of *Flying* magazine. It was the October issue, nearly six months old. It was the annual Naval Aviation issue. And in an article entitled "Life on a Carrier," on page 248, was this paragraph: "It's a mighty good feeling to know that even if you were shot down in Tokyo harbor, the Navy would be in to get you." It had never happened when that piece was written. That's prophecy.

The rescue ship radioed us the next day that Buchanan was feeling fine, and that just to be impartial they had also rescued another Navy pilot, a disgruntled Jap pilot, and a lone bedraggled survivor of a Jap picket boat!

• • •

I learned it wasn't the first time Ensign Buchanan and Lieutenant Fecke had seen exciting times together. The previous fall, off Formosa, a flight of seventy Jap planes pounced on two of our cruisers that were crippled. Fecke was leading a flight of eight of which Buchanan was one. Those eight took on the seventy Japs. They shot down twenty-nine of them, lost only one plane, broke up the attack and saved the cruisers. Fecke and Buchanan each got five Jap planes in that one foray. And each got the Navy Cross for the job. So the little Tokyo Bay incident didn't rattle them.

When I first saw Lieutenant Fecke I said to myself, "There's a Westerner for sure." I liked him before I ever really knew him. He just had that weather-beaten, cowboy look. And then he fooled me by turning out to be a New Englander, Massachusetts born, and a New Hampshire University graduate, in a business course at that. (He was twenty-six.) But he had the Westerner's trait of steadiness. He was very quiet and polite, he knew how to handle things, and he never got excited. Altogether he had shot down seven planes. The others described him as a man you'd like to have along if you ever got into trouble. To which Ensign Buchanan would undoubtedly say "Amen!"

The night after our strike on the southern islands, everybody was relaxed and had that wonderful sense of relief over the finish of a dangerous job. They showed a movie for the first time in three or four days. It was a western called *The Lights of Old Santa Fe*, with a regulation hero and villain and runaway horses and shootin' and everything. Those fliers received it the way modern audiences receive *The Drunkard*. We almost hissed the villain off the screen. We booed at all underhand business, we cheered all good deeds, and we whistled and clapped when the hero took the girl in his arms.

I think we enjoyed it more than any other movie on the whole trip.

The pilot who first shot down a Jap plane on our trip was Ensign Frank Troup, of Decatur, Alabama. It was a reconnaissance plane, and he got it the day before we reached Tokyo waters. It was his fifth, and it made him an ace. Troup said the only reason he got it was that he happened to be closer to it than his wing mates when they all spotted it. The boys who flew the patrols said that when they spotted a single Jap plane, everybody in the patrol opened wide, and it was just like a horse race to see who got within shooting distance first. That time it was Troup.

Next in line to Troup was Ensign Bob Hickle, of 146 Santa Ana Street, Long Beach, California. Hickle had gradually worked into the category of "always a bridesmaid, but never a bride." He and Troup had been together three times, and Troup had always got a plane. Hickle joked, "Now that Troup has got five, he'll have to start helping me get some." And the very next morning Hickle came back glowing; he had got his first plane. Yes, Troup was with him, but Hickle got it all by himself, without any help. I asked Hickle how it felt, and he said that he was so excited and anxious that he almost ran into the pieces when the Jap turned over in the air and exploded.

Among others of my pilot friends was Lieutenant Pleas Greenlee, of Shelbyville, Indiana, the executive officer of the fighter squadron. He was rather short, pleasant-faced, sucked at a pipe and always wore house slippers around the ship. He had one Jap plane to his credit. Before I knew his first name or where he was from, I asked him if he was any relation to Pleas Greenlee, a prominent Hoosier whom I'd met several times in Indiana.

"Yes," said the fighter pilot, "he's my father!"

Young Greenlee was an Annapolis graduate. His wife and baby girl were in Shelbyville and he had color photos of them all over his cabin. He was spending his spare time right then making a piggy bank out of a coconut for his little daughter.

Ensign Herbert Gidney, Jr., of 623 Devonshire Street, Pittsburgh, was a torpedo-bomber pilot who was making his first combat strike when he flew over Tokyo. He said he was so engrossed in doing everything just right that he wasn't scared at all. Gidney was a big fellow. He had gone to Lehigh University, and you'd have sworn he was a football player. But, no, his great love was skiing. He used to take trips way up into New England to ski, and he even walked as though he was on skis! Gidney had a system of letter writing I'd never seen before. He figured the only way to get letters was to write them. So he wrote sixteen letters a week – exactly sixteen. He had a list of sixteen people, made out on a big sheet of paper like a scoreboard, and he checked each one off as he finished the letter.

Lieutenant Howard Skidmore, another torpedo-bomber pilot, was from Villa Grove, Illinois. When he told me, I said, "Why, that's where my mother was born." Then I got to thinking I was mistaken; she was born at Carmargo, a few miles south. And now I'm not sure. At any rate Lieutenant Skidmore had lots of relatives around my home town of Dana, Indiana, and had been over there lots of times to see them. He had a strange experience on our ship. He was sitting in his plane with the engine running, just ready to start his takeoff. And at that moment a Jap bomb hit the deck, less than a dozen feet in front of Skidmore's plane. It killed several men and tore a big hole in the deck. Yet Skidmore wasn't scratched, and the close explosion didn't even deafen him or give him a headache.

When planes come back from a strike, they circle around their ship until they get the signal to land. Then they break out of formation one at a time into what is called the "landing circle." They try to space it so that one plane will be landed and clear of the barrier just as the next one approaches.

When an approaching pilot is about half a mile out, the landing signal officer begins giving him sign-language instructions. He is known as the LSO and he is one of the most important men on the ship. He is a flier himself, but his is no part-time job that is traded around among pilots. He has been especially trained, and this is his sole job.

The LSO stands on a platform just off the stern. Behind him is a large square of canvas which makes a background for his signals. Underneath the platform is a heavy rope netting, to catch him if he should fall off. He wears a yellow sweater and yellow helmet so that the incoming pilots can easily spot him. And in each hand is a paddle about twice the size of a ping-pong bat, either yellow or bright orange. These are his signal paddles.

From the moment the LSO starts his signals, the incoming pilot never takes his eyes off him. The LSO is actually flying the plane by remote control, and the pilot is only a robot who does what the LSO orders. By sign language, the LSO tells him he's too high or too low, too fast or too slow, that his tail hook isn't down, or a dozen other things. The pilot corrects for these mistakes as he approaches. If the correction is perfect, the LSO gives him the "cut" sign just before he reaches the flight deck. Instantly the pilot takes his eyes off the LSO and once more begins flying his own plane. Only half a dozen seconds are left. He has to act fast, and get that plane down. But, if the approach isn't quite right at the very last second, the LSO gives him a frantic "wave off" signal, and the pilot "pours on the coal," misses the deck by a scant few feet and goes around for another try. The LSO must decide at the last moment, actually in the fraction of a second, whether to let the pilot try it or not. I don't know of any situation that requires faster mind-making-up. You sure can't go into "conference" with anybody on that one.

The landing signal officer on our ship was a fine man named Lieutenant Bill Green, and he came from Newton, Iowa. He had graduated from a commercial course at the University of Iowa in 1942, and had won honorable mention for All-American that year. He intended to be a lawyer.

An LSO must first be a flier; second, he must be a man of steady nerves and sound judgment; and third, he must be a psychologist in a way, and know his pilots. Bill Green was all three. Everybody liked him and everybody had faith in him. It would be a sad bunch of pilots who had an incompetent LSO. Bill knew the flying traits of each pilot so well that he could identify every one merely by the movements of his plane, when he was still a mile from the ship!

Once, while watching our landings, I saw a pilot waved off seven times before he got in, and I asked Bill if that was a record. He said it certainly was not. A few months back he had to wave off a pilot twenty-one times before he finally got aboard. Which meant that one pilot was trying to land for almost two hours!

The landing signal officer's job is a precarious one. Many a time Bill had to duck, jump, or even run. The ship's photo lab had a marvelous picture of Bill actually being chased across the deck by a plane making a near-crash landing.

There is always an assistant on every carrier, in training to take over a regular job himself. Bill's assistant was Ensign Kal Porter, of Ogden, Utah. One day I got up my nerve, and went hack to stand with them while they landed a whole flight of planes. You'd have sworn every plane was going to land right on top of you. Before it was over I had decided that if I were running the Navy, I'd let them all land in the water.

One thing I had never understood about how an aircraft carrier operates is what they did with all the rest of the planes while one was landing or taking off. I had thought the flight deck had to be entirely clear, that as soon as one plane took off they brought the next one up from the lower deck by elevator and sent it off.

It isn't that way at all. There are always idle planes standing on deck during landings and takeoffs. There have to be, for the hangar deck down below isn't big enough to hold all the planes. But these idle planes are never along the side of the deck – they are at one end or the other.

Here's how it's done. Planes always take off and always land from stern to bow of the ship. For the takeoff, all the planes are parked tightly together at the rear of the deck. All have folding wings, a feature which has been one of the great contributions of this war. Without them a carrier could hardly carry enough planes to justify itself.

These parked planes take up perhaps one-eighth of the flight deck – the rear one-eighth. When they get ready to launch planes, all the engines are started and warmed up while the planes are still parked tightly together. The noise is terrific. Angry propellers whirl within inches of the tail of the next ship. Plane pushers by the dozen crawl around, under, and amidst these flying propellers, adjusting chocks and untying the lines that hold the planes down.

When they are ready, the center plane in the front row is taxied out a few feet. His folded wings are unfolded. The pilot tests his controls,

71

puts down his flaps. A signalman standing ahead and to the right of him indicates by motions when he is to start. He holds onto his brakes, speeds up his engine until the noise is ear-splitting, and then the signalman leans over and dramatically swings his arm forward, as though personally giving the plane impetus.

The plane starts rolling; seven-eighths of deck in front is clear – not a plane or man on it. No sooner has one plane gone than the next one is ready, has his wings unfolded, and is running up his engine. They take off one right after the other, less than a minute apart, until the whole flight is in the air.

The moment the last plane of the flight is off, a klaxon signals the fact, and the great flight deck instantly becomes a swarm of men. Usually there are several planes left on deck, which aren't scheduled to go. All these are immediately towed forward and reparked there, for, when the planes come back to land, they must use the rear end of the deck. While they are landing, the whole front end is full of parked planes. A barrier of steel cables, stretched head-high across the deck, stops any wild-landing plane from crashing into the bunch of tightly parked ships ahead.

As soon as a plane lands, the barrier is dropped, the plane taxies over it, and the barrier is raised again for the next man coming in. The plane that has just landed is parked among the others up front, and the pilot shuts off his engine. When the last plane is down, the klaxon squawks, all the men rush out, and the planes are towed back to the rear of the deck, ready for the next takeoff.

Almost never, during actual landing of the planes, is the elevator let down. It is used only between flights, to take planes down to the garage or bring up fresh ones.

This moving of planes from one end of the flight deck to the other is called "respotting." It goes on all day long-back and forth, back and forth. The planes are pulled by tiny Fordson tractors. As they run around they look like those little electric cars you bump each other with at carnivals.

At night, probably two-thirds of the planes are spotted on deck. They are parked tightly together, and tied down to gratings in the flight deck by heavy rope. If the ship is sailing into a storm, they're tied even more firmly with steel cable. And all night long men are posted among them, to see that nothing breaks or goes wrong.

Despite all this, there were times when the ocean was so rough and the deck dipping at such a steep angle that planes would break all their moorings and go screeching over the side. That would be when I was down in my cabin, very seasick.

CHAPTER FIVE

Love-day – Okinawa

I WAS aboard a troop transport and it was the evening before we stormed onto Okinawa. We were nervous. Anybody with any sense is nervous on the night before D-day. You feel weak and you try to think of things, but your mind stubbornly drifts back to the awful thought of tomorrow. It drags on your soul and you have nightmares. But such fears did not mean any lack of confidence. We would take Okinawa – nobody had any doubt about that. But we knew we would have to pay for it. Some on the ship would not be alive in twenty-four hours.

We were in convoy. Many, many big ships were lined up in columns with our warship escorts on the outsides. We were an impressive sight – yet we were only one of many similar convoys come from many different places. We had been on our way many days. We were the biggest, strongest force ever to sail in the Pacific – we were going into what we expected would be the biggest battle so far in the Pacific.

Our ship was an APA, or assault transport, and a war veteran. She had five stars on her service ribbon – Africa, Sicily, Italy, Normandy, and Southern France – and she wore the Purple Heart, Bronze Star, and Legion of Merit Silver Star. She had fared well on the other side and we hoped her luck would hold out in the Pacific. We were carrying marines. Some of them were going into combat for the first time;

others were veterans from as far back as Guadalcanal. They were a rough, unshaved, competent bunch of Americans. I was landing with them and I felt I was in good hands.

I shared a cabin with Marine Major Reed Taylor of Kensington, Maryland. He was a Guadal vet and he jokingly belittled newcomers who hadn't been through "Green Hell." The major and I were sort of two of a stripe and we got along fine. We had the nicest cabin either of us ever had at sea, and we took advantage of it by sleeping away almost the whole trip. We slept day and night, and so did many others. There was a daily argument as to whether or not one could store up sleep and energy for the ordeal ahead. The doctor said it was nonsense — a man can't store up sleep.

Between naps I read two books. They were Bob Hope's *I Never Left Home* (how I wish I never had!) and Bob Casey's *Such Interesting People*. Only I wished I could hear Bob Casey tell all those stories in person, lying on his cot in France and roaring and shaking with laughter. Bob's laughter would have been good for us then. A marine officer said, "I haven't laughed for three days."

Our trip had been fairly smooth and not many of the troops were seasick. Down in the holds the marines slept on racks four tiers high. It isn't a nice way to travel, but I never heard anybody complain. They came up on deck on nice days to sun and rest and wash clothes, or lie and read or play cards. We didn't have movies. The ship was darkened at sunset and after that there were only dim lights. The food was good. We got news every morning in a mimeographed paper, and once or twice a day the ship's officers broadcasted the latest news over the loud-speaker.

They kept us informed daily of the progress of the Okinawa bombardment that preceded our landing. Every little bit of good news cheered us. The ship, of course, was full of rumors, good and bad, but nobody believed any of them. Meetings were held daily among the officers to iron out last-minute details of the landing. Day by day, the marine troops were fully briefed on what they were to do.

Everything we read about Okinawa stressed that the place was lousy with snakes. It's amazing the number of people who are afraid of snakes. Okinawa "snake talk" cropped into every conversation.

On the last day we changed our money into newly manufactured "invasion yen," drew two days' K rations, took a last bath, and packed our kits before supper. We had a huge turkey dinner. "Fattening us up for the kill," the boys said. At three o'clock on the last afternoon there was a celebration of the Lord's Supper. It was the afternoon before Easter Sunday. A lot of us could not help but feel the tragic irony of it, knowing about tomorrow's battle.

For some reason which I never fathomed the conventional name of D-day was changed for that invasion to "Love-day." Possibly it was because we were landing on Easter Sunday and somebody felt the spirit of brotherly love. At any rate, when dawn came on Love-day and the pink, rising sun lifted the shroud of Oriental darkness around us, we were absolutely astonished. For all our main convoys had converged and there they lay around us in one gigantic fleet, stretching for miles. There were about 1,500 ships and thousands of small landing craft which the ships had carried with them. There weren't as many small ships as at Normandy, but in naval power and actual force of men and fighting strength it was equal to the invasion of Europe. We certainly didn't go at Okinawa in any halfhearted manner.

We had ham and eggs for breakfast at 4:30 a.m. We strapped our unwieldy packs on our backs, but heavier gear was left aboard to be taken ashore several days later. It was only half-light when we went on deck. The men on the deck were dark and indistinguishable forms. We could see flame flashes on the horizon toward shore.

Our assault transport carried many landing craft (LCVPs) on deck. A derrick swung them over the side, we piled into them as they hung even with the rail, and then the winch lowered them into the water. I went on the first boat to leave our ship. It was just breaking dawn when we left and still more than two hours before H-hour. Our long ocean trip was over. Our time had run out. This was it.

All around us hundreds of other boats were putting off and churning the water, but there was no organization to it. They weren't yet forming into waves. These early boats carried mainly the control crews who would manage the colossal traffic of shore-bound invasionists in the next few hours.

We chugged shoreward for more than an hour, for we had stopped far out. Our destination was a small control ship lying about two miles from the beach. Scores of these little control craft were forming a line the entire length of our long beachhead, about a quarter of a mile apart. They were the traffic policemen of our invasion. They all looked alike, and we had to find ours by number. In all the welter of ocean traffic it was easy to get lost, and we did. We were half an hour finding our control boat after getting to the line.

An assault on an enemy shore is a highly organized thing. It is so intricately organized that it would be impossible to clarify all the fine details. No single man in our armed forces knew everything about an invasion.

But, to simplify one thing, suppose we were invading an enemy beach on a four-mile front. It would not be one over-all invasion, but a dozen or more little invasions, going on simultaneously side by side. Each combat team runs its own invasion, and a combat team is a regiment. Our regimental commander and his staff were on the little control ship, directing only the troops of our regiment.

We had beaches "Yellow One" and "Yellow Two." Troops of our regiment formed waves directly off those beaches, miles at sea, and we went straight in. Other control ships on either side, having nothing to do with us, directed other waves. Each was its own private little show.

As I've said before, war to an individual is hardly ever bigger than a hundred yards on each side of him. And that's the way it was with us at Okinawa.

An hour and a half before H-hour at Okinawa, our vast fleet began its final, mighty bombardment of the shore with its big guns. They had been at it for a week, but this was a concentration whose fury hadn't been approached before. The power of the thing was ghastly. Great sheets of flame flashed out from a battery of guns, gray-brownish smoke puffed up in a huge cloud, then the crash of sound and concussion carried across the water and hit you. Multiply that by hundreds and you had bedlam. Now and then the smoke from a battlewagon would come out in a smoke ring, an enormous one 20 or 30 feet across, and float upward with perfect symmetry.

Then came our carrier planes, diving on the beaches, and torpedo planes, carrying heavy bombs and incendiaries that spread deep-red flame. Smoke and dust rose up from the shore, thousands of feet high, until finally the land was completely veiled. Bombs and strafing machine guns and roaring engines mingled with the crash of naval bombardment and seemed to drown out all existence. The ghastly concussion set up vibrations in the air – a sort of flutter – which pained and pounded the ears as though with invisible drumsticks. During all this time the waves of assault craft were forming up behind us.

The water was a turmoil of movement: dispatch and control boats running about, LSMs and LSTs moving slowly forward to their unloading areas, motor torpedo boats dashing around as guides. Even the destroyers moved majestically across the fleet as they closed up for the bombardment of the shore. From our little control ship and the scores like it, waves of assault craft were directed, advised, hurried up, or slowed down.

H-hour was set for 8:30. By 8 a.m. directions were being radioed and a voice boomed out to sea to form up waves 1 and 2, to hurry up, to get things moving. Our first wave consisted solely of heavy guns on amphibious tanks which were to get ashore and blast out the pillboxes on the beaches. One minute behind them came the second wave – the first of our foot troops. After that, waves came at about 10-minute intervals. Wave 6 was on its way before wave 1 ever hit the beach. Wave 15 was moving up before wave 6 got to the beach. That's the way it went.

We were on the control boat about an hour. I felt miserable and an awful weight was on my heart. There's nothing whatever romantic in knowing that an hour from now you may be dead.

Some officers I knew came aboard. They weren't going ashore until afternoon and they wanted to talk. I simply couldn't carry on a conversation. I went below to use a civilized toilet for the last time in many days. I got a drink of water, though I wasn't thirsty. Then one sailor came up and introduced himself and said he read the column, and a knot of sailors gathered around on deck.

One sailor with black, close-cropped hair and glasses offered me a cigar. I didn't even have the wit to put down his name. I told him I didn't smoke cigars, but I would take one for our regimental colonel, who practically lived on cigars and was about out of them. A few minutes later the sailor came up with five more cigars to give to the colonel. They wanted to give me candy, cigarettes, and cookies, but I told them I already had plenty.

Word came by radio that waves 1 and 2 were ashore without much opposition and there were no mines on the beaches. So far, so good. We looked at the shore through binoculars. We could see tanks moving across the fields and the men of the second wave walking inland, standing upright. There were a few splashes in the water at the beach, but we couldn't make out any real fire coming from the shore.

It was all very indefinite and yet it was indicative. The weight began to lift. I wasn't really conscious of it, but I found myself talking more easily with the sailors and somehow the feeling gradually took hold of me that we were to be spared. The 7th wave was to pick us up as it came by. I didn't even see it approaching. Suddenly they called my name and said the boats were alongside. I grabbed my pack and ran to the rail. I'm glad they came suddenly like that. The sailors shouted, "Good luck!" over and over and waved us off. We were on our way.

The LCVP was so crowded the men just stood against each other. I knew most of them, for they were all from the ship that brought us up. They had been riding for an hour before they picked us up off the control boat and they were soaked to the skin from the spray. The morning was warm and sunshiny, yet they were all very cold from being wet. Some of them got the cold shakes which wouldn't stop, and they joked with each other about quaking with fear instead of cold. We all smiled in a sickly sort of fashion. We talked most of the way, but I can't remember much of what we said.

These Pacific islands have one bad feature that we never had to contend with in any of the European invasions — a reef that lies just under water three or four hundred yards out. A boat of any size can't run up to the beach, for it can't get over the reef; consequently, we had to transfer again about a half mile from shore. We ran up alongside a fleet of amphtracks — amphibious tractors — which were waiting there for us. These are like big trucks, only they're on tractors. When in the water the tractor treads, built cup-like, propel the thing along. The moment it touches bottom it crawls along like a tractor. It can go miles to sea or miles inland.

Our packs were so heavy it was hard to get from one boat to the other and it took our load about ten minutes to transfer. And then we started the last lap, the one that really counted.

The terrific bombardment had completely stopped about a minute before H-hour. By now almost an hour had passed and the ships were again firing, spasmodically. Small fires were burning inland and a great cloud of black smoke rose from the airport, up on high ground. But the pall of smoke and dust that had covered the beach had blown away and we could clearly see the men on shore and the wave ahead of us landing.

We had all expected to go onto the beach in a hailstorm of tracer bullets, mortar shells throwing sand, and artillery shells whistling into the water near us. And yet we couldn't see a bit of firing ahead. We hoped it was true. While we were hoping, somebody took out his canteen and had a drink. People get thirsty as they approach a beachhead. The canteen went around. When it came to me I took a big gulp, and almost choked. For it wasn't water at all but straight brandy!

During the bombardment and all during the landings a lone four-engined Liberator bomber flew slowly back and forth over the beach. We marveled at his audacity, for he seemed an easy target for ack-ack. Yet he didn't seem to get shot at. Liberators are too big for carriers to handle, so it would have had to come all the way from the Philippines or Iwo Jima or Saipan. We presumed it carried photographers. It seemed incongruous, lumbering around up there alone so nonchalantly. We were musing on the Liberator when suddenly the amphtrack hit bottom, tilted way over on one side as though it was going to upset, then tilted back with a big thump that almost threw us off our feet. We were crossing the coral reef. It was a good crossing at that; the water was smooth and there were no rollers on the reef.

From the reef on in, the amphtrack joggled and tilted as it rode the rough coral bottom. Then at last it climbed out of the water and onto the sand. We ran up about twenty feet from the water's edge and the driver let down the ramp that forms the rear end of the amphtrack.

We stepped out. We were on Okinawa an hour and a half after H-hour without getting shot at and we hadn't even got our feet wet. The first words I heard on Japanese soil were from an incredulous marine who said, "Hell, this is just like one of MacArthur's landings."

We had landed absolutely unopposed, which is indeed an odd experience for a marine. It was incredible; nobody among us had dreamed of such a thing. We all thought there would be slaughter on the beaches. There was some opposition to the right and to the left of us, but on our beach, nothing, absolutely nothing.

We didn't expect that to continue, of course — a marine doesn't fool himself like that. Certainly there would be hard fighting ahead and we all had our fingers crossed. But to get the firm foothold we had, with most of our men ashore and our supplies rolling in, was a gift for which we were grateful.

It was a beautiful day. One of the marines, after spending months in the tropics, remarked, "This weather feels more like American weather than anything since I left home."

It was sunshiny and very warm and there was no wind. We had heard it would be cold and many of the boys wore heavy underwear and were now sweating and regretting. I wore two pairs of pants, but I soon took off one of them. We were dressed in green herringbone combat uniforms. Everybody had made the trip in khaki and changed that morning aboard ship, leaving their old khaki lying on their bunks to be collected by the Navy, cleaned, and used to clothe prisoners and our own casualties who lost their clothes.

We brought ashore only what we could carry on our backs. When we put on our new green fatigues, one marine remarked, "The latest Easter style — herringbone twill."

I had dreaded the sight of the beach littered with mangled bodies, and my first look up and down the beach was a reluctant one. Then like a man in the movies who looks away and then suddenly looks back unbelieving, I realized there were no bodies anywhere — and no wounded. What a wonderful feeling!

In fact, our entire regiment came ashore with only two casualties: one was a marine who hurt his foot getting out of an amphibious truck; the other was, of all things, a case of heat prostration! And to add to the picnic atmosphere, they had fixed me up with a big sack of turkey wings, bread, oranges, and apples. So instead of grabbing a hasty bite of K rations for our first meal ashore, we sat and lunched on turkey wings and oranges.

There were caves in the low chalky cliffs on the island, and in the caves were brick-colored urns a couple of feet high. These urns contained the ashes of many honorable ancestors. Our bombardment had shattered a lot of these burial vaults. What our big guns had missed, the soldiers and marines took a precautionary look into by prying off the stone slabs at the entrances.

In front, looking out to sea, stood our mighty fleet with scores of little black lines extending to shore – our thousands and thousands of landing craft bringing more men and big guns and supplies. And behind me, not two feet away, was a caveful of ex-Japanese. Which is just the way it should have been. A nice Easter Sunday, after all.

Never before had I seen an invasion beach like Okinawa. There wasn't a dead or wounded man in our whole sector of it. Medical corpsmen were sitting among their sacks of bandages and plasma and stretchers, with nothing to do.

There wasn't a single burning vehicle, nor a single boat lying wrecked on the reef or shoreline. The carnage that is almost inevitable on an invasion was wonderfully and beautifully not there.

There was hardly anybody at all on the beach when we landed. The few assault waves ahead of us had pushed on inland, and all that vast welter of people and machines that make a beach hum with work were still many waves behind us. The bulldozers and the jeeps had not yet arrived. There was no activity and hardly any sound. It was almost as though we were the original explorers.

Our little party, which was the regimental staff, moved to the foot of a bluff about 100 yards back of the beach. It was full of caves and our naval gunfire had made a rubble at the foot of the bluff. But several cave mouths still gapped open. We decided to set up there until the colonel could get the picture in his mind, through information brought by runners, of just what was going on.

There were about a hundred men with us in addition to the officers. The men were under First Sergeant Andy Anderson, from Washington State. The first thing Andy had them do was to make sure there were no Japs hiding in the caves to snipe on us, for the first waves had gone through too fast to clean everybody out – if anybody had been there. So they would sneak up on a hole, with rifles ready, and Andy would take out a hand grenade and throw it into the hole. But the first one hit the edge of the hole and rolled down outside. Andy threw himself on the sand and all the rest of us lay flat. The grenade went off with a bang, but nobody got hurt. From then on we kidded Andy about the fine display of marine marksmanship he had given us.

In addition to being great fighters, I believe the marines are the friendliest bunch I've ever been with. I've never had any trouble with people being unfriendly, but marines seem to have it bred into them to be pleasant and to make you feel at home.

Nothing like Okinawa had ever happened to them before. They were accustomed to butchery on the beaches. They'd kept saying to me, "If you could just have been with us before, we'd have shown you some excitement."

And I would reply, "Brother, I've had all the excitement I need for a lifetime. This kind of invasion suits me fine."

I started wandering up and down the beach. One boy was carrying a little vase in his hand, saying, "Here's the first souvenir of Okinawa!" He was James Cosby, pharmacist first class, of Cereal Spring, Illinois. He had found the vase lying outside one of the burial vaults.

Then I noticed a tall and heavily laden marine, carrying a roll of telephone wire on his shoulders and leading a white nanny goat by a string. I stopped him and said, "Would you like to have you and your goat in the newspapers?"

He grinned and said, "Sure. Why not?"

He was Pfc. Ben Glover of Baird, Texas. He had been a telephone lineman at home, and that's what he was there. Linemen were always among the first ashore.

By evening of Love-day, scores of marines had baby goats for pets and were leading them around. There were lots of goats on Okinawa and the little ones were so white and so cute that we animal-loving Americans couldn't resist adopting them. I saw one marine who had commandeered a horse and had it carrying his pack. Another had a bicycle. By Love-day Plus 3, I was sure they would be carrying little Japanese babies on their backs. Americans are the damnedest people! Why can't everybody be like them?

Actually Okinawa doesn't look very different from most of America. In fact it looked much more like America than anything the marines had seen for the last three years. The climate is temperate rather than tropical, and so is the vegetation. There are tropical trees on and near the beaches – I think they're pandanus bushes – but there are also many trees of the fir family with horizontal limbs.

The country over which my regiment passed during the first two days was cultivated. It rose gradually from the sea in small fields and it didn't look at all unlike Indiana in late summer when things have started to turn dry and brown, except that these fields were much smaller. The wheat, which looked just like ours, was dead-ripe in the fields now; the marines cut it with little sickles. In other fields there were cane and sweet potatoes.

Fields have ditches around the edges, and dividing them are little ridges about two feet wide. On top of the ridges are paths. All through the country are narrow dirt lanes and now and then a fairly decent gravel road. As you get inland, the country becomes rougher. In the hills there is less cultivation and more trees. It is really a pretty country; we had read about what a worthless place Okinawa was, but I think most of us were surprised at how pretty it was.

The Okinawa civilians we brought in were pitiful. The only ones left seemed to be very old or very young and they all were very, very poor. They were not very clean personally, and their homes were utterly filthy. Over and over I heard marines say, "This could be a nice country if the people weren't so dirty."

Obviously their living standard is low. Yet I've never understood why poverty and filth need to be synonymous. A person doesn't have to be well off to get clean, but apparently he has to be well off to want to keep clean. We've found it that way clear around the world. The people were dressed as we see Japanese dressed in pictures: women in kimonos and old men in skin-tight pants. Some wore a loose, knee-length garment that showed their skinny legs. The kids were cute as kids are all over the world; I noticed marines reaching out and tousling their hair as they marched past them. We rounded up all the civilians and put them in camps and they were puzzled by it all.

Most of the farm families must have got out when our heavy bombardments started. Lots of farmhouses had either been demolished or burned to the ground before we came. Often, in passing a wrecked farmhouse, we smelled the sickening odor of death inside. But there are always people who won't leave, no matter what. We couldn't help feeling sorry for the Okinawans we picked up in the first few days. We found two who spoke a little English. They had once lived in Hawaii. One was an old man who had a son (Hawaiian-Japanese) somewhere in the American Army!

They were all shocked from the bombardment and I think they were rather stupefied too; when they talked they didn't make much sense. I don't believe they had any idea of what it was all about. As one marine officer said, "The poor devils. I'll bet they think this is the end of the world."

They were obviously scared to death. The marines found many of them hiding in caves. They found two old women, seventy-five years old or more, in a cave caring for a paralyzed girl. One of the old ladies had a small dirty sack with some money in it. She cried and tried to give the marines the money — hoping, I suppose, that she could buy herself off from being executed. After all the propaganda they had been fed about our tortures, they were a befuddled bunch of Okinawans when they discovered we had brought right along with us, as part of the intricate invasion plan, enough supplies to feed them too!

During our first afternoon on Okinawa my group of marines went about a mile and a half inland. Our vehicles were not ashore yet, so we had to pack on our backs everything we had. I myself was overladen as usual. I had two canteens, a musette bag, a blanket rolled up in a poncho, three rubber life preservers, a shovel, and assorted knives, first-aid kits, etc. Furthermore, I was carrying two jackets and an extra pair of pants, and it was hotter than hell.

The result of all this was that for the first time in my life I couldn't keep up. I hated to do it, but I had to sit down now and then to rest and let the others go ahead. (A lifetime of sin and crime finally docs catch up with you.) Anyhow, we finally got where we were going. We stopped on a hillside, threw down our gear, connected our phones to wires on the ground, and were ready for business. That is, the others were. I lay down on the grass and rested for an hour.

After that we began getting ready for the night. We figured the Japs would bomb us all night, that their artillery would soon start up from the hills, and that when it got dark some slinky infiltrators would start infiltration. So we dug foxholes. The slope was so steep I chose a nice depression at the foot of a small embankment that didn't require much digging.

Now we come to the life preservers. You may have wondered why I was carrying three lifebelts on dry land. Well, I knew what I was doing all right. I just blew up my three life preservers, spread them in the foxhole, and I had the nicest improvised Simmons you ever saw. We finally got onto that trick after a few invasions in Europe and all one summer in France I slept comfortably on three blown-up preservers. It was worth the struggle of carrying them just to see the reaction of the marines. They would come up to look at this strange device and stand there, staring, and then say, "Well, I'll be damned. Why in the hell couldn't I have thought of that!"

Then we got out our K rations and my friend, Major Reed Taylor, came and squatted Indian-fashion while I made hot coffee for us with some new heat tablets the marines had issued. By the time we finished it was almost dark.

Everybody who wasn't on guard at the edge of our little camp, or who wasn't standing duty at the field telephones, went to bed, for in Jap country you don't move around at night unless you have to. Going to bed was merely a figure of speech for everybody except me. I seemed to be the only one who had brought a blanket and I definitely was the only one who had nice soft life preservers to sleep on. The others slept on the ground in their foxholes with their ponchos wrapped around them. A poncho is wind- and waterproof, but it has no warmth. In fact, it seems to draw all the warmth out of your body and transmit it into the air.

Our first night on Okinawa was uncanny and full of old familiar sounds — the exciting, sad, weary little sounds of war. It had been six months since I'd slept on the ground, or heard a rifle shot.

We were on a pretty, grassy slope out in the country. The front lines were about a thousand yards ahead and other troops were bivouacked all around us. There were still a few snipers hiding around. An officer was brought in just before dark, shot through the arm, so we were on our toes.

Just at dusk three planes flew slowly overhead in the direction of the beach. We paid no attention, for we thought they were ours. But they weren't. In a moment all hell cut loose from the beach. Our entire fleet and the guns ashore started throwing stuff into the sky. I'd never seen a thicker batch of ack-ack. As one of the marines said, there were more bullets than there was sky. Those Jap pilots must have thought the world was coming to an end when they flew into that lead storm only ten hours after we had landed on Okinawa. All three were shot down.

As deep darkness came on, we got into our foxholes and settled down for the night. The countryside became as silent as a graveyard — silent, that is, between shots. The only sounds were war sounds. There were no country sounds at all. The sky was a riot of stars.

Captain Tom Brown was in the foxhole next to me. As we lay there on our backs, looking up into the starry sky, he said, "There's the Big Dipper. That's the first time I've seen that since I've been in the Pacific." The marines of this division had done all their fighting under the Southern Cross, where our Big Dipper doesn't show.

As full darkness came, flares began lighting the country ahead of us over the front lines. They were shot in shells from our battleships, timed to burst above our lines, and float down on parachutes. That was to keep the country lighted up so we could see the Japs if they tried to infiltrate, which was one of their favorite tricks. The flares were shot up at the rate of several per minute, from dusk until the moon came out full. It was so bright after that that flares were not needed.

All night long two or three ships kept up a slow shelling of the far hills where the Japs were supposed to be. It wasn't a bombardment – just two or three shells per minute. They passed right over us, and I found that passing shells have the same ghostly "window-shade rustle" on this side of the world as on the other.

My foxhole was only about twenty feet from where two field telephones and two field radios were lying on the ground. All night, officers sat there, directing our troops with these four pieces of communication. As I lay there listening in the dark, the conversation was startling familiar – words, thoughts, and actions exactly as I'd known them for so long in the infantry. Throughout the night I could hear these low voices in the darkness, voices of men running the war at the front.

Shortly after dark the rifle shots started, first a little flurry far ahead, maybe a dozen shots, then silence for many minutes. Then came another flurry, way to the left, and again silence. Now the closer blurt of a machine gun, and a few scattered single shots sort of framing it. Then another long silence. Spooky. It was like that all night; flares in the sky ahead, the crack of big guns behind us, the whine of passing shells, the few dark figures coming and going, muted voices at the telephones, the rifle shots, the stars, the feel of the damp night air under the wide sky.

I was back again at the kind of life I had known so long. It was the old familiar pattern, unchanged by distance or time from war on the other side of the world – a pattern so embedded in my soul that, coming back to it again, it seemed to me as I lay there that I'd never known anything else in my life. And there are millions of us.

The day had been hot, but the night got mighty cold and a very heavy dew came gradually, soaking everything. All the others practically froze and got very little sleep but for once in my life I was as warm as a bug. Yet I didn't sleep very much. There's always a flaw somewhere and in this case it was mosquitoes. I'd never been so tortured by them. They were persistent. They were tenacious. And they were the noisiest mosquitoes I'd ever associated with. They were so noisy that when I pulled the blanket over the side of my face and covered my cars tight I could still hear them. I doused my face twice with the mosquito repellent that the marines issued, but it did no good whatsoever. It was eleven o'clock before I finally got asleep. At 2 a.m. I awakened and knew something was wrong. It was my face. My upper lip was so swollen I thought I had a pigeon egg under it. My nose was so swollen the skin was stretched tight over it. And my left eye was nearly shut. After that I just went under the blanket and decided to suffocate. I did sleep that way, but the next morning I was groggy and dopey from sleeping without air.

Those mosquitoes really put a scare into me. I had heard that Okinawa was malarial and I certainly got enough mosquito venom that night to give malaria to half of California. So, bright and early, I started taking atabrine for the first time in my life.

CHAPTER SIX

Men from Mars

AFTER a short time with the headquarters of the marine regiment, I moved to a company and lived and marched with them for several days. The company was a part of the First Marine Division. I introduced myself to the company commander who took me on a half hour's walking trip around the company area before leaving me with the men. They had turned in for the night and put out perimeter defenses so that no infiltrating Japs could get through and also so that any big attack could be dealt with. The company was on a hill about 300 yards long and 100 yards wide. The men were dug in down the sides of the hill and there was a mortar platoon at the foot, all set up to throw mortars in any direction.

Our part of the island had not then been declared "secured," and we had received warning of possible attacks from sea that night. Nobody was taking any chances. "This is the most perfect defensive position we've ever had in our lives," the company commander said. "One company could hold off a whole battalion for days. If the Japs had defended these hills they could have kept us fighting for a week."

The company commander was Captain Julian Dusenbury from Claussen, South Carolina, a young man with a soft southern voice. His black hair was almost shaved and he was a little yellow from taking atabrine. He was easy-going with his men and you could tell they liked him. It happened that his twenty-fourth birthday was on April 1 – the Easter Sunday we landed on Okinawa. His mother had written that she hoped he'd have a happy birthday. "That was the happiest birthday present I ever had," he said, "going through Love-day without a single casualty in the company."

Captain Dusenbury said I could have my choice of two places to spend the first night with his company. One was with him in his command post, a big, round Japanese gun emplacement made of sandbags. The Japs had never occupied it, but they had stuck a log out of it, pointing it toward the sea so that to aerial reconnaissance it looked like a gun. Captain Dusenbury and a couple of his officers had spread ponchos on the ground inside the emplacement, had hung their telephone on a nearby tree and were ready for business. There was no roof on the emplacement. It was right on top of a hill and cold and very windy.

My other choice was with a couple of enlisted men who had room for me in a little gypsy-like hide-out they'd made. It was a tiny, level place about halfway down the hillside and away from the sea. They'd made a roof for it by tying ponchos to trees, and in a farmhouse they had found some Japanese straw mats which they'd spread on the ground. I chose the second of these two places, partly because it was warmer, and also because I wanted to be with the enlisted men.

My two "roommates" were Corporal Martin Clayton, Jr., of 3400 Princeton Street, Dallas, Texas, and Pfc. William Gross of 322 North Foster Street, Lansing, Michigan. Clayton was nicknamed "Bird Dog" and nobody ever called him anything else. He was tall, thin, and dark, almost Latin looking. He sported a puny little mustache he'd been trying to grow for weeks, and he made fun of it. Gross was simply called Gross. He was very quiet, and thoughtful of little things, and both of them looked after me for several days. The two of them had become very close friends, and after the war they intended to go to UCLA together to finished their education.

The boys said we could all three sleep side by side in the same "bed." So I got out my contribution to the night's beauty rest, and very much appreciated it was, too. Those marines had been sleeping every night on the ground with no cover, except for their cold, rubberized ponchos, and they had almost frozen to death. Their packs were so heavy they hadn't been able to bring blankets ashore with them. But I had carried a blanket as well as a poncho.

Our next-door neighbors, about three feet away, had a similar level spot on the hillside, and they had also roofed it with ponchos. These two men were Sergeant Neil Anderson of Coronado, California, and Sergeant George Valido of Tampa, Florida. So we chummed up and the five of us made a fire and cooked supper under a tree just in front of our "house."

Other little groups of marines had fires going all over the hillside. As we were eating, another marine came past and presented Bird Dog with a big piece of fresh roasted pig they had just cooked. Bird Dog gave me some and it sure was good after days of K rations. Several of the boys found their K rations moldy, and mine were too. They were the old-fashioned kind and we finally decided they were the 1942 rations which had been stored, probably in Australia, all this time.

Suddenly, from a few yards downhill, we heard somebody yelling and cussing, and then there was a lot of laughter. One marine had heated a ration can and, because it was pressure packed, it blew up when he pried it open and sprayed hot egg yolks over him. Usually the boys opened a can a little before heating to release the pressure so that it couldn't explode.

After supper we burned our ration boxes on the fire, brushed our teeth with water from our canteens, and then just sat talking on the ground around the fire. Other marines drifted along and after a while there were more than a dozen sitting around. We smoked cigarettes and talked of a hundred things. The first topic was, as in all groups, about our surprise at no opposition to our landing. Then they got to asking me what I thought about things over here and how it compared with Europe. And when did I think the war would end? Of course, I didn't know any of the answers but it made conversation. The boys told jokes, they cussed a lot, they dragged out stories of their past blitzes, and they spoke gravely about war and what would happen to them when they finally got home.

We talked like that for about an hour, and then it grew dark and a shouted order came along the hillside to put out the fires. It was passed on and on, and the boys drifted away to their own foxholes or hillside dugouts, and Bird Dog, Gross, and I went to bed. There was nothing else to do after dark in blackout country.

That was one of the most miserable damn nights out of hundreds of miserable nights I ever spent in this war. It was too early to go to sleep, so we just lay there in the dark and talked some more. You could hear voices faintly all over the hillside. We didn't take off our clothes, of course; nobody does in the field. I did take off my boots but Bird Dog and Gross left theirs on since they had to stand watch on the field telephones from 1 till 2 a.m. The three of us lay jammed up against each other, with Bird Dog in the middle. We smoked one-cigarette after another. We didn't have to hide them under the blanket since we were in a protected position where a cigarette couldn't be seen very far.

The mosquitoes started buzzing around our heads. Okinawa mosquitoes sound like flame throwers; they can't be driven off or brushed away. I got a little bottle of mosquito lotion out of my pocket and doused my face and neck, though I knew it would do no good. The other boys didn't even bother. After a while the hillside grew silent. The hours went past. By an occasional slap at the mosquitoes each of us knew the others weren't asleep.

Suddenly Bird Dog sat up and pulled down his socks and started scratching. The fleas in the grass were after him. For some strange reason I am immune to fleas. Though half the boys had red welts from hundreds of itchy little flea bites, I have never had one. But I'm the world's choicest morsel for mosquitoes. Every morning I woke up with at least one eye swollen shut.

That was the way it was all night — me with a double dose of mosquitoes and the rest with a mixture of mosquitoes and fleas. You could hear marines softly cussing all night long around the hillside. Suddenly there was a terrific outburst just downhill from us and a marine came jumping out into the moonlight, swearing and jerking at his clothes. "I can't stand these goddam things any longer," he cried. "I've got to take my clothes off."

We all laughed under our ponchos while he stood there in the moonlight and stripped off every stitch, even though it was very chilly. He shook and brushed his clothes, doused them with insect powder, and then put them back on. This unfortunate soul was Corporal Leland Taylor of 101 Francis Court, Jackson, Michigan. He was thirty-three years old and his nickname was Pop. Pop was a "character." He had a black beard and even in the front lines he wore a khaki overseas dress cap, both of which made him conspicuous. After Pop went back to bed everything was quiet for several hours, but hardly anybody was asleep. The next morning the boys on guard said that Pop must have smoked three packs of cigarettes that night. It was the same way with Bird Dog, Gross, and me.

One of the boys on guard came to wake my bedmates at a quarter to one, but they weren't asleep. I thought I might get to sleep while they were away, but I didn't. The mosquitoes were really crucifying me. The boys came back about two o'clock, took off their shoes and lay down. With my blanket over the three of us we were as warm as toast; at least we had that.

All night, without even raising our heads, we could see flashes of the big guns of our fleet across the island. They were shelling the southern part and shooting flares to light up the front lines there. Sometimes we could actually see red-hot shells, traveling horizontally the whole length of their flight, ten miles away from us, and then we saw them explode. Every so often throughout the night our own company's mortars were called upon to shoot a flare over the beach behind us, just to make sure nothing was coming in.

Once there was a distinct rustling of the bushes in front of us. Of course the first thing I thought of was a Jap, but immediately I figured a Jap wouldn't make that much noise and I decided it was one of the horses the mortar boys had commandeered, crashing through the bushes. And that's what it turned out to be.

Pop Taylor also had the Jap idea, at first. The next morning "Brady" Bradshaw, who was sleeping with Pop, said Pop shook him violently during the night to wake him up and borrow a .45, just in case. Brady laughed and laughed about it, for lying on the ground between them all the time was an arsenal of two carbines, two shotguns, and Pop's own .45.

Along about 4:30 I guess we did sleep a little from sheer exhaustion. That gave the mosquitoes a clear field. When we woke up at dawn and crawled stiffly out into the daylight, my right eye was swollen shut, as usual.

All of which isn't a very warlike night to describe, but there are lots of things besides bullets that make war hell.

We started moving right after breakfast. We were to march about a mile and a half, then dig in and stay in one place for several days, patrolling and routing out the few hidden Japs in that area. We were in no danger on the march – at least we thought we weren't, and not all the marines wore steel helmets. Some wore green twill caps, some baseball caps, some even wore civilian felt hats they had found in Japanese homes. For some reason soldiers the world over like to put on odd local headgear. I've seen soldiers in Italy wearing black silk opera hats, and over here I've seen marines in combat uniform wearing panama hats. I've always enjoyed going along with an infantry company on the move, even some of the horrible moves we had to make in Italy and France. But that morning it was a really pleasant one. It was early and the air was good. The temperature was perfect and the country was pretty. We all felt that sense of ease that comes of knowing nothing too bad is ahead of you. Some of the boys were even smoking cigars.

There were always funny sights in a moving column of soldiers. Our mortar platoon had commandeered a dozen local horses to carry heavy pieces. One of the marines had tied the pack onto his horse with a Japanese obi – one of those reams of sash Japanese women wear on their backs. There he was, dirty and unshaved, leading a sorrel horse with a big bow-tie of black and white silk, three feet wide, tied across its chest, and another one tied under its belly, the ends standing out on both sides.

Troops carry the oddest things when they move. One marine had a Jap photo album in his hand. One had a wicker basket. Another had a lacquered serving tray. They even had a Columbia phonograph with

Jap records, strapped onto a horse. Many of them wore Japanese insignia or pieces of uniform. Later an order came out that any marine caught wearing Jap clothing would be put on burial detail. Maybe that was to keep marines from shooting each other by mistake.

There were frequent holdups ahead of us and we would stop and sit down every hundred yards or so. One marine, commenting on the slow progress, said: "Sometimes we take off like a ruptured duck, and other times we just creep along." The word was passed down the line, "Keep your eyes open for planes." About every sixth man turned his head to repeat it, and the word was sent back along the column like a wave. Toward the rear it came out: "Keep your eyes open for planes – keep your eyes open for cabbages – keep your eyes open for geisha girls."

We were walking almost on each other's heels, a solid double line of marines. Bird Dog was behind me. He said, "A column like this would be a Jap pilot's delight."

Another said, "If a Jap pilot came over the hill, we'd all go down like bowling pins." But no Japs came.

At one of our halts the word came back that we could sit down, but we were not to take off our packs. From down the line came music, a French harp and ukulele playing "You Are My Sunshine." When it was finished the marines called back request numbers. The little concert went on for five or ten minutes out there in the Okinawa fields. The harmonicist was Pfc. William Gabriel, a bazookaman from a farm on Rural Route 13, about ten miles out of Houston, Texas. He was only nineteen, but a veteran who had sustained one wound. He was a redhead and the shyest soldier I'd ever met, so bashful he could hardly talk. But he surely could make a harmonica talk. Playing with him on a sort of ukulele common to Okinawa was an officer, Lieutenant "Bones" Carsters of 6023 Miramar Boulevard, Los Angeles. It was an instrument with three strings, its head made of tightly stretched snakeskin. It gave me the willies just to look at one.

When we started ahead again, the way was clear and that time we went like the well-known ruptured duck and after about a mile we arrived, all panting.

When I saw my first Jap soldiers it was mid-forenoon and we had just reached our new bivouac area. The boys threw off their packs, sat down on the ground, and took off their helmets to mop their perspiring foreheads. We were in a small grassy spot at the foot of a hill. Most of the hillsides had caves in which household stuff was hidden. They were a rich field for souvenir hunters, and all marines are souvenir hunters. So immediately two of our boys, instead of resting, started up through the brush, looking for caves and souvenirs. They had gone about fifty yards when one of them yelled, "There's a Jap soldier under this bush."

We didn't get too excited, since most of us figured he meant a dead Jap. But three or four of the boys got up and went up the hill. A few moments later somebody else yelled, "Hey, here's another one. They're alive and they've got rifles."

The boys went at them in earnest. The Japs were lying under two bushes, with their hands up over their cars and pretending to be asleep. The marines surrounded the bushes and, with guns pointing, ordered the Japs out. But the Japs were too scared to move. They just lay there, blinking.

The average Jap soldier would have come out shooting, but, thank goodness, these were of a different stripe. They were so terrified the marines had to go into the bushes, lift them by the shoulders and throw them out in the open. My contribution to the capture consisted of standing at one side and looking as mean as I could.

One Jap was small, about thirty years old. The other was just a boy of sixteen or seventeen, but good-sized and well built. He had the rank of superior private and the other was a corporal. They were Japanese from Japan, and not the Okinawan home guard. They were both trembling all over. The muscles in the corporal's jaw were twitching. The kid's face was a sickly white and he was so paralyzed he couldn't even understand sign language.

We never knew why those two Japs didn't fight. They had good rifles and potato-masher hand grenades. They could have stood behind their bushes and heaved grenades into our tightly packed group and got themselves two dozen casualties, easily. The marines took their arms. One marine tried to direct the corporal in handbook Japanese, but the fellow couldn't understand. The scared kid just stood there, sweating like an ox. I guess he thought he was dead. Finally we sent them back to the regiment.

The two marines who flushed the Japs were Corporal Jack Ossege of Silver Grove, Kentucky, across the river from Cincinnati, and Pfc. Lawrence Bennett of Port Huron, Michigan. Okinawa was the first blitz for Bennett and these were the first Jap soldiers he'd ever seen. He was thirty years old, married, and had a baby girl. Back home he was a freight dispatcher.

The Jap corporal had a metal photo holder like a cigarette case in which were photos that we took to be of three Japanese movie stars. They were pretty, and everybody had to have a look.

Ossege had been through one Pacific blitz, but this was the first time he had ever taken Japs alive. He was an old hand at souvenir hunting and he made sure of getting a Jap rifle. That rifle was the envy of everybody; later, when we were sitting around discussing the capture, the other boys tried to buy or trade him out of it. Pop Taylor offered him $100 for it, and the answer was no. Then Taylor offered four quarts of whisky. The answer still was no. Then he offered eight quarts. Ossege weakened a little. He said, "Where would you get eight quarts of whisky?" Pop said he had no idea. So Ossege kept the rifle.

It's wonderful to see a bunch of American troops go about making themselves at home wherever they get a chance to settle down for a few days. My company dug in at the edge of a bomb-shattered village. The village was quaint and not without charm. I was astonished at its similarity to the villages of Sicily and Italy, for it didn't really seem Oriental. The houses were wooden one-story buildings, surrounded by little vegetable gardens. Instead of fences, each lot was divided by rows of shrubs or trees. The cobblestoned streets, winding and walled head-high on both sides, were just wide enough for a jeep.

A large part of the town lay shattered. Scores of the houses had been burned, and only ashes and red roofing tile were left. Wandering around, I counted the bodies of four Okinawans still in the street. Otherwise the town was deserted. The people had fled to their caves in the hillsides, taking most of their personal belongings with them.

There is almost no furniture in Japanese houses, so they didn't have to worry about that.

After a few days the grapevine carried the news to them that we were treating them well, and they began to come out in droves to give themselves up. I heard one story about a hundred Okinawa civilians who had a Jap soldier among them; when they realized the atrocity stories he had told them about the Americans were untrue, our MPs had to step in to keep them from beating him.

Our company commander picked out a nice little house on a rise at the edge of town for his command post. The house was very light, fairly clean, and the floors were covered with woven straw mats. A couple of officers and a dozen men moved in and slept on the floor, and we cooked our rations over an open stone cookstove in the rear.

Then the word went around for the men of the company to plan to stay for several days. Two platoons were assigned to dig in along the outer sides of the nearby hills for perimeter defense. The boys were told they could keep the horses they had commandeered, that they could carry wooden panels out of the houses to make little doghouses for themselves, but not to take anything else. And they could have fires, except during air alerts.

They weren't to start their daily mop-up patrols in the brush until the next day, so they had the afternoon off to clean themselves up and fix up their little houses. Different men did different things. Some built elaborate homes about the size of chicken houses, with floor mats and chairs and kerosene lanterns hanging from the roof. One Mexican boy dug a hole, covered it with boards, and then camouflaged it so perfectly with brush you couldn't really see it. Some spent the afternoon taking baths and washing clothes in the river. Others rode bicycles around town, or rode their horses up and down. Some foraged around town through the deserted houses. Some went looking for chickens to cook. Some sat in groups and talked. Some just slept.

An order eventually went out against wearing Jap clothing or eating any of the local vegetables, pork, goat, beef, or fowl. But before the order came, some marines had dug up lots of Japanese kimonos out of the smashed houses and put them on while washing their single set of clothes. It was a funny sight – those few dozen dirty and unshaved marines walking around in women's pink and blue kimonos. A typical example was Private Raymond Adams of Fleason, Tennessee. He had fixed himself a dugout right on the edge of a bluff above the river, with a grand view and a nice little grassy front yard. There he had driven stakes and built a fire, over which he hung his helmet like a kettle, and he was stewing a chicken. He had taken off his clothes and put on a beautiful pink-and-white kimono.

Later a friend came along with a Jap bicycle minus one pedal, and Adams tried without much success to ride it up and down a nearby lane. If there ever is a war play about marines I hope they include one tough-looking private in a pink-and-white kimono, stewing chicken, and trying to ride a one-pedaled bicycle through a shattered Japanese village. Private Adams was married and had an eight-month-old son he had never seen. If the baby could have seen his father that day he would probably have got the colic from laughing.

When I was aboard ship somebody walked off with my fatigue and combat jackets, so I was given one of those Navy jackets lined with fleece. It was much warmer and nicer than what I'd had. On the back it had stenciled in big white letters: U. S. Navy. I wore it when I first walked through the company's defense area and later that evening, when we were sitting on the ground around a little fire warming our supper of K rations. By that time I'd got acquainted with a good many of the boys and we felt at home with one another.

We had some real coffee which we poured into our canteen cups, and we sat around drinking it before dark. Then one of the boys started laughing and said to me, "You know, when you first showed up, we saw that big Navy stencil on your back and after you passed, I said to the others: 'That guy's an admiral. Look at the old gray-haired bastard. He's been in the Navy all his life. He'll get a medal out of this, sure as hell.' "

The originator of this bright idea was Pfc. Albert Schwab of 1743 East 14th Street, Tulsa, Oklahoma. He was a flame thrower, and flame throwers have to be rugged guys, for the apparatus they carry weighs about seventy-five pounds and also they are very apt to be shot at by the enemy. But to see Albert sitting there telling that joke on himself and me, you'd never have known he was a rugged guy at all. I'm not an admiral and I won't get any medal, but you do get a lot of laughs out of this war business when things aren't going too badly.

One morning after breakfast about a dozen of us were sitting on the mat-covered floor talking things over while sipping our coffee. Several days' accumulation of grime covered everybody. Suddenly Bones stood up and said, "I cleaned my fingernails this morning and it sure does feel good."

And then my friend Bird Dog held his own begrimed hands out in front of him, looked at them a long time, and said, "If I was to go to dinner in Dallas and lay them things up on a white tablecloth I wonder what would happen."

A good many of the Okinawan civilians wandering along the roadside bowed low to every American they met. Whether this was from fear or native courtesy I do not know, but anyhow they did it. And the Americans, being Americans, usually bowed right back.

One of my marine friends got mixed up in one of those little bowing incidents. He was Pfc. Roy Sellers, a machine gunner from Amelia, Ohio. Roy was married and had a little girl two years old. He used to be a machinist at the Cincinnati Milling Machine Company and he played semi-pro ball too. When Roy had a beard he looked just like a tramp in a stage play. He was only twenty-seven, but looked much older; in fact he went by the nickname "Old Man."

On this occasion Old Man was trying to ride a Japanese bicycle along the bank of a little river where we camped. The ground was rough and the bicycle had only one pedal and Roy was having a struggle to keep it upright. Just then an old Okinawan, bareheaded and dressed in a black kimono and carrying a dirty sack, walked through our little camp. He wasn't supposed to be at large but it was none of our business and we didn't molest him. He was bowing to everyone, right and left, as he passed. Then he met Machine Gunner Sellers on his one-pedaled bicycle. Roy was already having his troubles, but as he came abreast of the Okinawan, he bowed deeply over the handle bars, hit a rut, lost his balance, and over he went. The Okinawan, with Oriental inscrutability, returned the bow and never looked back.

We all laughed our heads off. "Who's bowing to whom around here?" we asked. Roy denied he had bowed first, but we knew better. He decided to give his old bicycle away to somebody less polite than himself.

As our company was moving forward one day I looked down the line of closely packed marines and I thought for a moment I was back in Italy. There for sure was Bill Mauldin's cartoon character of GI Joe – the solemn, bearded, dirty, drooping, weary old man of the infantry. This character was Pfc. Urban Vachon of French-Canadian extraction, who came from Laconia, New Hampshire. He had a brother, William, fighting in Germany. Urban was such a perfect ringer for Mauldin's soldier that I asked the regimental photographer to take a picture of him to send back to the States. If you've seen it, you can prove to any disbelievers that soldiers do look the way Mauldin made them look.

We camped one night on a little hillside that led up to a bluff overlooking a small river. The bluff dropped straight down for a long way, and up there on top it was just like a little park, terraced, although it wasn't farmed, and the grass was soft and green, with small, straight-limbed pine trees dotted all over it. Looking down from the bluff, the river made a turn. Across it was an old stone bridge at the end of which was a village – or what had been a village. Now it was just a jumble of ashes and sagging thatched roofs. In every direction little valleys led away from the turn in the river – as pretty and gentle a sight as you ever saw. It had the softness of antiquity about it and the miniature charm and daintiness typical of Japanese prints. And the sad, uncanny silence that follows the bedlam of war.

A bright sun made the morning hot, and a refreshing little breeze sang through the pine trees. There wasn't a shot or a warlike sound within hearing. I sat on the bluff for a long time, just looking. I noticed a lot of the marines sitting and just looking too.

You could come from a dozen different parts of America and still find scenery on Okinawa that looked like your country at home.

Southern boys said the reddish clay and the pine trees reminded them of Georgia. Westerners saw California in the green rolling hills, partly wooded, partly patchworked with little green fields. And the farmed plains looked like our Midwest.

Okinawa is one of the few places I've been in this war where our troops didn't gripe about what an awful place it was. In fact, most of the boys said they would like Okinawa if it weren't at war with us and if the people weren't so dirty. The countryside is neat and the little farms are well kept. At the time the climate was superb and the views undeniably pretty. 'Hie worst crosses to bear were the mosquitoes, the fleas, and the sight of the pathetic people.

Most of the roads on Okinawa were narrow dirt trails for small horse-drawn carts, but there were several wider gravel roads. One man aptly described it as "an excellent network of poor roads." Our heavy traffic, of course, played hob with the roads; already they were tire-deep in dust and traveling troops had masklike faces, caked with dust. Bulldozers and scrapers were constantly at work.

I've mentioned before our fear of snakes before we got to Okinawa. All the booklets given us ahead of time dwelt at length on snakes, telling us that there were three kinds of adders, all of them fatally poisonous. We were warned not to wander off the main roads, not to stop under the trees lest snakes drop on us. (As if you could fight a war without getting off the roads!) Some of the troop briefings had the marines more scared of snakes than of Japs.

I kept a close watch and made a lot of inquiries, and found that in the central part of Okinawa where we were there are practically no snakes at all. Our troops walked, poked, sprawled, and slept on nearly every square yard of the ground. And in my regiment, for one, only two snakes were seen. One was found dead; the other was killed by a battalion surgeon who coiled it into a gallon glass jar and sent it to the regimental command post as a souvenir. It was a vicious rattler, a type called habu.

Those were the only snakes I heard of. There was a rumor that in one battalion they caught and made pets of a couple of snakes, but I didn't believe it. The local people said the island was full of snakes up until the middle thirties when some mongooses were imported which killed most of them. But we didn't see any mongooses, so we didn't know whether the story was true or not. Correspondent John Lardner said his only explanation was that St. Patrick came through here once as a tourist and took all the snakes with him.

Leland Taylor, the marine corporal known as 'Pop,' found four pairs of the most beautiful Japanese pajamas you ever saw in a wicker basket hidden in a cave. They were apparently brand-new, had never even been worn. They were thrilling to look at and soft to the touch. Pop carried the basket around on his arm from place to place until he could get a chance to ship them home to his wife.

One morning I wandered down to our mortar platoon and ran into a young fellow with whom I had a great deal in common. We were both from Albuquerque and we both had mosquito trouble. He was Pfc. Dick Trauth of 508 West Santa Fe Street. Both his eyes were swollen almost shut from mosquito bites, and at least one of mine was swollen shut every morning. We both looked very funny. Dick still was just a boy. He'd been nineteen months in the marines and a year overseas – a veteran of combat and still only seventeen years old. Dick wrote letters to movie stars and Shirley Temple had sent him a picture, autographed to his company just as he asked her to do. Dick was very shy and quiet and I had a feeling he must be terribly lonesome, but the other boys said he wasn't and that he got along fine.

One of the marines who drove me around in a jeep whenever I had to go anywhere was Pfc. Buzz Vitere of 2403 Hoffman Street, Bronx, New York. Buzz had other accomplishments besides jeep driving; he was known as the Bing Crosby of the Marine Corps. If you shut your eyes and didn't listen very hard you could hardly tell the difference. I first met Buzz on the transport coming up to Okinawa. He and a friend gave an impromptu concert on deck every afternoon. They would sit on a hatch in the warm tropical sun and pretty soon there would be scores of marines and sailors packed around them, listening in appreciative silence. It made the trip to war almost like a Caribbean luxury cruise.

Buzz's partner was Pfc. Johnny Marturello of 225 Livingston Street, Des Moines, Iowa. Johnny played the accordion. He was an Italian, of course, and had the Italian Hair for the accordion. He sang too, but he said as a singer his name was "Frank Not-so-hotra." Johnny played one piece he composed himself – a lovely thing. He sent it to the GI Publishing Co., or whatever it was in the States, and I feel positive if it could be widely played it would become a hit. The piece is a sentimental song called "Why Do I Have to Be Here Alone?" Johnny wrote it for his girl back home, but he grinned and admitted they were "on the outs."

Johnny went ashore on Love-day and his accordion followed two days after. In his spare moments he sat at the side of the road and played for bunches of Okinawans whom the marines had rounded up. They seemed to like it. Johnny had a lot of trouble with his accordion down south in the tropical climates. Parts would warp and stick and mildew, and he continually had to take the thing apart and dry and clean it, but it was worth the trouble. It kept Johnny from getting too homesick. He knew the accordion would probably be ruined by the climate, but he didn't care. He brought it along with him from America just for his own morale. "I can always get a new accordion," Johnny said, "but I can't get a new ME."

Nearly two years back when I was with Oklahoma's Forty-fifth Division in Sicily and later in Italy, I learned they had a number of Navajo Indians in communications.

When secret orders had to be given over the phone these boys gave them to one another in Navajo. Practically nobody in the world understands Navajo except another Navajo. My regiment here had the same thing. There were about eight Indians who did this special work. They were good marines and very proud of it.

There were two brothers among them, both named Joe. Their last names were different; I guess that's a Navajo custom, though I never knew it before. One brother, Pfc. Joe Gatewood, went to the Indian school in Albuquerque. In fact, our house is on the very same street, and Joe said it sure was good to see somebody from home. Joe had been out in the Pacific for three years; he had been wounded and been

105

awarded the Purple Heart. He was thirty-four and had five children back home he wanted to see.

Joe's brother was Joe Kellwood who had also been in the Pacific three years. A couple of the others were Pfc. Alex Williams of Winslow, Arizona, and Private Oscar Carroll of Fort Defiance, Arizona, which is the capital of the Navajo reservation. Most of the boys were from around Fort Defiance and used to work for the Indian Bureau.

The Indian boys knew before we got to Okinawa that the invasion landing wasn't going to be very tough. They were the only ones in the convoy who did know it. For one thing they saw signs, and for another they used their own influence.

Before the convoy left the far south tropical island where the Navajos had been training since the last campaign, the boys put on a ceremonial dance. The Red Cross furnished some colored cloth and paint to stain their faces and they made up the rest of their Indian costumes from chicken feathers, sea shells, coconuts, empty ration cans, and rifle cartridges. Then they did their own native ceremonial chants and dances out there under the tropical palm trees with several thousand marines as a grave audience. In their chant they asked the great gods in the sky to sap the Japanese of their strength for this blitz. They put the finger of weakness on the Japs, and they ended their ceremonial chant by singing the Marine Corps song in Navajo.

I asked Joe Gatewood if they really felt their dance had something to do with the ease of our landing and he said the boys did believe so and were very serious about it, himself included. "I knew nothing was going to happen to us," Joe said, "for on the way up here there was a rainbow over the convoy and I knew then everything would be all right."

One day I was walking through the edge of a rubbled Okinawa village where marine telephone linemen were stringing wire to the tops of the native telephone poles. As I passed, one of the two linemen at the top called down rather nervously that he was afraid the wobbly pole was going to break under their weight; to which one of the men on the ground, apparently their sergeant, called back reassuringly,

"You've got nothing to worry about. That's imperial Japanese stuff. It can't break."

There are very few cattle on Okinawa, but there are many goats and horses. The horses are small like western ponies and mostly bay or sorrel. Most of them are skinny, but if they are well fed they are good-looking horses. They are all well broken and tame. The marines acquired them by the hundreds; our company alone had more than twenty. The boys put their heavier packs on them; more than that, they just seemed to enjoy riding them up and down the country roads. They rigged up rope halters and one marine made a bridle using a piece of bamboo for a bit. They dug up old pads and even some goatskins to use as saddle blankets. Rut it was surprising how many men in a company of marines didn't really know how to ride a horse.

There was one very small marine who was as nice as he could be, always smiling and making some crack. The boys said that in battle he didn't give a damn for anything. The first afternoon I joined his company he didn't know who I was and as we passed, he said very respectfully, "Good evening, colonel." I had to chuckle to myself. Later he mentioned it and we laughed about it and then he started calling me Ernie.

He was Corporal Charles Bradshaw of 526 South Holmes Avenue, Indianapolis. Though only nineteen he was on his third campaign in the Pacific. He had had three pieces of shrapnel in him and from time to time they would try to work out through the skin. One was just about to come out of his finger.

In the Marines, Corporal Bradshaw was called "Brady" for short. Before joining up he worked on a section gang for the Pennsylvania Railroad. He usually wore one of those wide-brimmed green cloth hats instead of the regulation marine cap and he always carried a .45. It had a slightly curved 25 cent piece embedded in the handle – as he said, "to make it worth something."

In a cave Brady found two huge photograph albums full of snapshots of Japanese girls, Chinese girls, young Japs in uniform, and family poses. He treasured it as though it were full of people he knew. He studied it for hours and hoped to take it home with him. "Anything for a souvenir" could be the motto of the Marine Corps.

Another Indianapolis marine I met on Okinawa was Pfc. Dallas Rhude of 1437 East Raymond Street, who used to be a newspaperman. He worked on the Indianapolis Times; he started carrying it as a newsboy when he was eight, then got into the editorial room as a copy boy and kept that job till he joined the Marine Corps. He was a replacement; in other words, he was in the pool from which the gaps made by casualties are filled. But since there had been very few casualties he hadn't replaced anybody yet. Dallas spent twenty-two months in Panama, was home for a little while, and now had been in the Pacific for four months. He said that the Okinawa climate sure beat Panama.

Marines may be killers, but they're also just as sentimental as anybody else. I had talked with one pleasant boy in our company but there was no little incident to write about him, so I hadn't put his name down. The morning I left the company and was saying goodby all around, I could sense that he wanted to tell me something, so I hung around until it came out. It was about his daughter, born about six weeks back. This marine was Corporal Robert Kingan of 2430 Talbot Avenue, Cuyahoga Falls, Ohio. He had been a marine for thirteen months and in the Pacific seven months. Naturally he had never seen his daughter, but he had a letter from her!

It was a V letter written in a childish scrawl and said: "Hello, daddy. I am Karen Louise. I was born February twenty-fifth at four minutes after nine. I weigh five pounds and eight ounces. Your Daughter, Karen."

And then there was a P.S. on the bottom: "Postmaster – Please rush. My daddy doesn't know I am here."

Bob didn't know whether it was his wife or his mother-in-law who wrote the letter. He thought maybe it was his mother-in-law – Mrs. A. H. Morgan – since it had her return address on it. So I put that down and then asked Bob what his mother-in-law's first name was. He looked off into space for a moment, and then started laughing. "I don't know what her first name is," he said. "I just always called her Mrs. Morgan!"

The major part of the battle was being fought by the Army – my old friends, the doughfoots. This time the marines had it easy. Marine Corps blitzes in the Pacific had all been so bitter and the men had fought so magnificently that I had conjured up a mental picture of a marine as someone who bore a close resemblance to a man from Mars. I was almost afraid of them. I did find them confident, but neither cocky nor smart-alecky. They had fears, and qualms, and hatred for war the same as anybody else. They wanted to go home just as badly as any soldiers I've ever met. They are proud to be marines and they wouldn't be in any other branch of the service, yet they are not arrogant about it. And I found they have a healthy respect for the infantry.

One day we were sitting on a hillside talking about the infantry. One marine spoke of a certain division – a division they had fought beside – and was singing its praises. "It's as good as any marine division," he said.

"What was that you said?" a listener cut in.

The marine repeated it and emphasized it a little. Another marine stood up and called out, loudly, 'Did you hear what he said? This guy says there's an army division as good as any marine division. He must be crazy. Haw, haw, haw!"

And yet other boys chimed in, arguing very soberly, and sided with the one who had praised the army division.

Before I came into the field, several marine officers asked me to try to sense just what the marine spirit is, what is its source, and what keeps it alive. In peacetime when the Marine Corps was a small outfit, with its campaigns highlighted, everybody was a volunteer and you could understand why they felt so superior. But with the war the Marine Corps had grown by hundreds of thousands of men. It became an outfit of ordinary people – some big, some little, some even draftees. It had changed, in fact, until marines looked to me exactly like a company of soldiers in Europe. Yet that Marine Corps spirit still remained. I never did find out what perpetuated it. The men were not necessarily better trained, nor were they any better equipped; often they were not so well supplied as other troops. But a marine still considered himself a better soldier than anybody else, even though nine-tenths of them didn't want to be soldiers at all.

They were very much aware of the terrible casualties they'd had in this Pacific war. They were even proud of that too, in a way. Any argument about superiority among units was settled by citing the greatest number of casualties. Many of them even envisioned the end of the Marine Corps at Okinawa. If the marine divisions had been beaten as they were on Iwo Jima, the boys felt it would have been difficult to find enough men of Marine Corps caliber to reconstitute all the divisions. They even had a sadly sardonic song about their approach to Okinawa, the theme of which was "Goodby, Marines!"

The boys of my regiment were continuously apologizing to me because the Okinawa campaign started out so mildly. They felt I might think less of them because they didn't show me a blood bath. Nothing could have been further from the truth. I was probably the happiest American there about the way it turned out for us. I told them that kind of campaign suited me, and without exception they came back with the answer that it suited them too. I heard it said so many times that it almost became a chant: "If they could all be like this, we wouldn't mind war so much."

No, marines don't thirst for battles. I've read and heard enough about them to have no doubts whatever about the things they can do when they have to. They are o.k. for my money, in battle or out.

CHAPTER SEVEN

L'Envoi

OUR war with Japan has gone well in the last few weeks. We are firmly on Okinawa, which is like having your foot in the kitchen door. Our wonderful carrier pilots have whittled down the Jap air force daily. Our antiaircraft from ships and from shore batteries has plugged Jap fliers for the highest ratio I've ever known from ack-ack. Our task forces have absolutely butchered the only Jap task force put to sea in many months. B-29s are hitting Japan, with fighter escorts from Iwo Jima. Airfields are springing up on Okinawa. We all say we sure are glad we are not in the Japs' shoes.

One main question asked over here now is, "How long will the Japs hold out?" There are all kinds of opinions, but nobody really knows. We don't know because no one in his right mind can pretend to understand the Oriental manner of thinking. They are unpredictable. They are inconsistent. As one officer said, "They are uncannily smart one day, and dumb as hell the next."

Their values are so different from ours. The news broadcasts from Tokyo and Shanghai are an example. These broadcasts are utterly ridiculous. During our first week here they constantly told of savage counterattacks when there weren't any. They told of driving a large part of our landing forces back to the boats and far out to sea, whereas actually they fired only a few shots onto the beaches. On D-day Plus 4, they broadcast that despite their counterattacks we finally succeeded in landing 6,000 troops. The truth is that by sunset of the first evening we had scores of thousands of Americans on Okinawa!

Everything that Tokyo said about us was a downright lie. Yet maybe Tokyo really believed it. No one can tell. The Japs don't think as we do.

The crippled Jap air force can do only spasmodic harm from now on, and their navy needn't ever be considered. If you could see the colossal naval power we have here you would hardly believe your eyes. It's one of the most impressive things I've seen in this war. We have plenty of troops in reserve, and new convoys of supplies began to arrive just as we finished unloading the original massive supply fleet.

The majority of the Japs are on the southern tip of the island, and in considerable strength. The northern area is being combed and a few scattered ones mopped up. There is tough fighting in the south and it will remain tough to the end. I've heard some officers say the south end may turn into another Iwo Jima. That will mean heavy casualties on our side, but the end of Okinawa is inevitable.

And while the Army's 24th Corps of Infantry is doing that job, the rest of the island apparently is wide open for us to develop and we are doing it with our usual speed. This island has everything we could want in such an island. There is plenty of room for more airfields, room for roads and vast supply dumps and anchorages for ships. And the civilians from whom we had expected trouble are docile and harmless. The way Americans can build, this island can be transformed in two months. Before long it could look like Guam or Pearl Harbor. We are in Japan's back door and while we are here they can't really do very much to us.

Of course, Japan's vast land armies are still almost intact. But if it docs come to the great mass land warfare of continental Europe, we now are able to build up strength for that warfare right on the scene. There is a fighting spirit among us. People are conjecturing about the possibility of the Pacific war's ending sooner than we had ever allowed ourselves to think. For years it looked endless, but now you hear people talk about being home maybe by Christmas. Some really believe they will. Others have their fingers crossed, but they are more hopeful than ever before.

Instead of a war weariness, there seems to be a new eagerness among our forces to sweep on and on, and wind the thing up in a hurry.

Photographs

Two days before Ernie left Guam this picture was taken by Captain Edward J. Steichen, USNR.

"The climate is good, the islands are pretty, and the native Chamorros arc nice people."

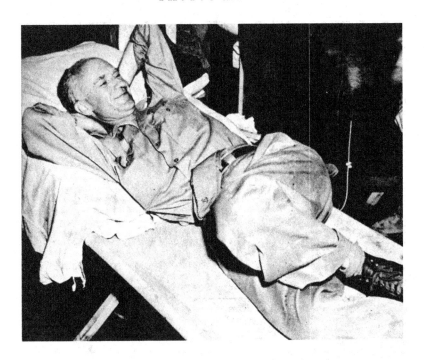

"There's no city and no place to go. If you got a three day pass you'd probably spend it lying on your cot."

"There's no city and no place to go. If you got a three day pass you'd probably spend it lying on your cot."

Waiting for the plane which will take hint to join the fleet. Ernie has a cup of coffee and a chat at a Naval Air Transport Terminal.

"My carrier was part of that first strike on the Tokyo area and we helped out at Iwo Jima, too."

"She was known in the fleet as 'The Iron Woman' because she had fought in every battle in the Pacific in 1944 and every one to date in 1945."

Aboard a troop transport on the way to Okinawa; "Our trip had been fairly smooth and not many of the troops were seasick."

"We were carrying Marines. Some of them were going into combat for the first lime. Others were veterans from as far back as Guadalcanal. They were a rough, unshaven, competent bunch of Americans. I was landing with them. I felt I was in good hands."

After the landing—"Say, aren't you Ernie Pyle?" I said, "Right," and he said "Whoever thought we'd meet you here? I recognized you from your picture."

"One main question asked over here now is, 'How long will the Japs hold out?'"

Near a Command post of the Third Marine Division he meets "Jeep" a scout and security patrol Doberman Pinscher.

"After a couple of days with the headquarters of the marine regiment I moved to a company and lived and marched with them for several days."

My company dug in at the edge of a bomb-shattered village. The village was quaint and not without charm. . . . The houses were wooden one-story buildings surrounded by little vegetable gardens.

"The old familiar pattern, unchanged by distance or time . . . a pattern so imbedded in my soul that it seemed I'd never known anything else in my life. And there are millions of us."